GERMAN U-BOAT ACES

Karl-Heinz Moehle
Reinhard Hardegen
Horst von Schroeter

GERMAN U-BOAT ACES

Luc Braeuer

Karl-Heinz Moeßle
Reinhard Hardegen
Horst von Schroeter

The Incredible
Patrols of U-123
in World War II

SCHIFFER MILITARY

4880 Lower Valley Road   Atglen, PA 19310

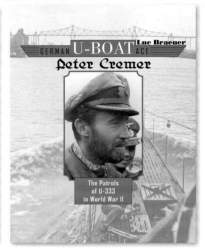

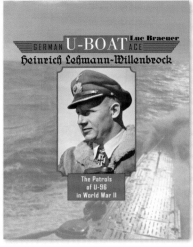

**German U-boat Ace
Rolf Mützelburg**
The Patrols of U-203
in World War II
Luc Braeuer.

Size: 9" x 12"
240 color and b/w images • 88 pp
ISBN: 978-0-7643-4835-8
hard cover • $29.99

**German U-boat Ace
Adalbert Schnee**
The Patrols of U-201
in World War II
Luc Braeuer.

Size: 9" x 12"
206 color and b/w images • 96 pp
ISBN: 978-0-7643-4823-5
hard cover • $29.99

**German U-boat Ace
Peter Cremer**
The Patrols of U-333
in World War II
Luc Braeuer.

Size: 9" x 12"
215 color and b/w images • 80 pp
ISBN: 978-0-7643-5071-9
hard cover • $29.99

**German U-boat Ace
Heinrich Lehmann-Willenbrock**
The Patrols of U-96
in World War II
Luc Braeuer.

Size: 9" x 12"
230 color and b/w images • 80 pp
ISBN: 978-0-7643-5401-4
hard cover • $29.99

Schiffer books may be ordered from your local bookstore,
or they may be ordered directly from the publisher by writing to:
Schiffer Publishing, Ltd., 4880 Lower Valley Rd., Atglen, PA 19310
(610) 593-1777; Fax (610) 593-2002, E-mail: Info@schifferbooks.com

Copyright © 2019 by Schiffer Publishing Ltd.

Originally published as *U-Boote: L'incroyable odyssée du U-123*
by Zéphyr Edition © 2014 Zéphyr Edition, Paris

Translated from the French by Omicron Language Solutions, LLC

Library of Congress Control Number: 2019934823

Type set in Minion Pro/Bodoni MT/Zurich BT

ISBN: 978-0-7643-5866-1

Printed in China

Published by Schiffer Publishing, Ltd.

4880 Lower Valley Road

Atglen, PA 19310

Phone: (610) 593-1777; Fax: (610) 593-2002

E-mail: Info@schifferbooks.com

Web: www.schifferbooks.com

For our complete selection of fine books on this and related subjects, please visit our
website at www.schifferbooks.com. You may also write for a free catalog.

Schiffer Publishing's titles are available at special discounts for bulk purchases for sales
promotions or premiums. Special editions, including personalized covers, corporate
imprints, and excerpts, can be created in large quantities for special needs. For more
information, contact the publisher.

We are always looking for people to write books on new and related subjects. If you have
an idea for a book, please contact us at proposals@schifferbooks.com.

CONTENTS

Kapitänleutnant Karl-Heinz Moehle, U-123's first commander. *UBA*

Reinhard Hardegen, the second commander. *LB*

Horst von Schroeter, U-123's third commander. *UBA*

U-123, a long-range, IXB-type, oceangoing U-boat, was put into service on May 30, 1940. Before leaving for combat, it was used in making the film *U-Boote Westwärts* (*U-boats Westward!*). After three successful patrols in the North Atlantic, its first commander, Karl-Heinz Moehle, was awarded the Knight's Cross. After the fourth patrol, he accepted a job on land as chief of the 5th U-boat Flotilla in Kiel. The second commander, Reinhard Hardegen, had taken a naval officer and pilot course. Like his predecessor, he also took part in four particularly successful combat patrols. During the first patrol, he hunted as a lone wolf off the African coast, where he sunk five ships. On its arrival in Lorient in August 1941, U-123 had the honor to be the first boat to inaugurate the new Keroman I base. Just before Christmas 1941, it was sent with four other U-boats off the American coast to set off "Operation Drumbeat." On January 12, 1942, U-123 sank the first ship in American Atlantic waters. When it returned to Lorient a month later with ten victory pennants, its commander was decorated with the Knight's Cross by Admiral Karl Dönitz in person. Filmed, photographed, and interviewed—"I saw New York through my periscope"—Reinhard Hardegen became a national hero in Germany. He carried out a second mission off the American coast, during which he added another eleven victory pennants for eight ships sunk and three damaged. He added the Oak Leaves to his Knight's Cross and disembarked to take up a post in a training flotilla. U-123's third commander, Horst von Schroeter, named in June 1942, arrived at a very difficult time. He couldn't take advantage of numerous, lightly protected targets like his predecessors, who had patrolled during the two "golden times" for the German U-boat service, and the omnipresent Allied air cover made life hard. After four patrols he was awarded the Knight's Cross on June 1, 1944.

U-123 spent a total of 720 days at sea, of which 690 were combat patrols, which was considerable. Its operations took place in the North Atlantic to Canada, off the North and South American coasts, and in the Gulf of Guinea to Freetown in Africa. During its twelve combat patrols, it sank forty-two freighters for a total of 219,924 tons, as well as two warships for 3,892 tons, and damaged five other merchant ships and a warship for 53,568 tons, which put it as the third most successful U-boat. U-123 escaped from twenty Allied attacks, both marine and aerial. Returning unscathed but in a sorry shape to Lorient in the spring of 1944, it was one of the rare U-boats to survive the war. After changing its flag, it took up service in the German navy for eleven years under the name of submarine *Blaison*. Apart from the book written by Hardegen in 1942, no other work has been written about it until now. The photos that illustrate its patrols come from U-Boot Archiv in Cuxhaven, and from the author's collection; he was able to represent the missions of the last commander thanks to the personal photo album of the U-boat's IWO *Leutnant zur See* Wolf-Harald Schüler.

U-123 when it arrived in Kiel on May 29, 1942, with three rows of pennants and the number 304,975—corresponding to tons of Allied ship announced as sunk—painted onto the conning tower. *UBA*

U-123, built in the Deschimag AG Weser shipyard in Bremen, was put into service on May 30, 1940. Before leaving for combat, the U-boat was taken to Kiel, Danzig, and then Gotenhafen (now Gdynia). During two and a half months out of these ports on the Baltic Sea, the crew carried out test dives, trained in firing the gun and launching torpedoes, and finally took part in simulated U-boat wolfpack attacks against artificial convoys. On August 15, 1940, once all these tests and exercises were finished, U-123 was put at the disposal of a UFA (Universum-Film Aktiengesellschaft) film crew for sixteen days of filming for the movie *U-Boote Westwärts!* On September 3, 1940, U-123 headed for the shipyard in Wilhelmshaven and faced its first dangers. The minesweeper that preceded it destroyed two floating mines in their path. Arriving in Wilhelmshaven, U-123 spent ten days in the shipyard undergoing complete careening and overhaul. On September 15, foodstuff and arms were loaded, which took three days. After having its hull demagnetized, U-123 was ready for combat.

May 30, 1940, at Bremen, the Deschimag AG Weser shipyard officially hands over U-123 to its first commander, *Kapitänleutnant* Karl-Heinz Moehle. Aged twenty-nine, this officer has already proved himself by sinking five ships as commander of the IIB-type U-20 during the first five months of World War II. *UBA*

The IXB-type U-123 measures 76.50 meters long and 6.80 meters wide. Its displacement is 1,051 tons on the water, and 1,178 submerged. It carries 165 tons of fuel, which gives it an autonomy on the surface of 8,700 miles at an average speed of 12 knots. Its antinetting protection on the front will be destroyed during firing tests with the 105 mm gun. *UBA*

Test dive. This U-boat has two 2,200 hp diesel motors, which allow it to reach a top speed of 18.2 knots on the surface, and two 500 hp electric motors for sailing up to 7.3 knots while submerged. The main disadvantages are that it is harder to maneuver and, above all, takes longer to dive than a VII type. *UBA*

Making the film *U-Boote Westwärts* took sixteen days. Several famous actors play the part of crew members, and *Konteradmiral* Karl Dönitz, head of the German U-boat Corps, played himself. On the left is the false commander, and on the right the real one. *UBA*

This film presents an imaginary and particularly successful combat mission: the U-boat returns with nine victory pennants flying from the periscope.

By mid-September 1940, U-123 is ready for combat. It is armed with a 105 mm gun, as well as six 553 mm torpedo-launching tubes—four in the fore and two aft. It can carry twenty-two torpedoes on missions, including those in reserve under the deck. *UBA*

A scene with the propellers caught in netting, and showing off the 20 mm antiaircraft gun in the "winter garden" behind the conning tower. Intended to encourage young men to engage in the U-boat Corps, this film will be shown in all the cinemas throughout Germany. *UBA*

A party to celebrate the end of filming, and fanciful decorations are distributed. *UBA*

First Ship on the "Hit List"

U-123 put out of Kiel in the early hours of September 21, 1940. On the twenty-ninth, after passing to the north of the British Isles, it reached its operating sector specified by U-boat service: the AL 6121 square west of Ireland. It was part of a line of several U-boats spread out to look for convoys. Because the sea was empty, it was sent to a new zone in the AL 5293 square, which it reached at 2000 hours on October 1. The following day, a radio message reported a convoy at about ten hours from its position, and U-123 moved farther west. At 1215 on October 6, after it had spent three unfruitful days searching, a steamer was spotted in the AL 7124 square; this was lagging behind the OB-221 convoy out of Liverpool. After approaching submerged, U-1223 fired its first torpedo against an Allied ship, at a distance of 1,650 meters. The 5,943-ton British freighter *Benlawers*, loaded with military materiel including trucks for Port-Said, sank in fifteen minutes: it was the first success. On October 9, a new convoy farther north was reported by U-103. U-123 managed to reach the back of it in the early hours of the following morning. During the day, the U-boat moved up the convoy, diving twice at 1230 and 1645 following the sudden appearance of a plane. At 1957, a steamer was spotted to port; the U-boat crash-dived, but suddenly the form of a destroyer appeared. This finally moved away and U-123 resurfaced at 2120. The freighter was still there and appeared to have stopped due to mechanical problems. It was a large ship about 140 meters long, heavily loaded and estimated at 7,500 tons. At 2134, a first torpedo set at a depth of 3 meters was fired, without results—it was obviously defective. A second torpedo was fired at 2144, and it exploded under the bridge, causing a cloud of smoke that rose to 150 meters into the air. The explosion took place after a trajectory of one minute, twenty-eight seconds, signifying that the target was at a distance of 1,320 meters. The ship sank in ten minutes; this was the 3,697-ton British freighter *Graigwen*. This ship, lagging behind the SC-6 convoy out of Canada for England, had already been damaged the night before by a torpedo from U-103.

At the end of September 1940, on watch west of Ireland. *UBA*

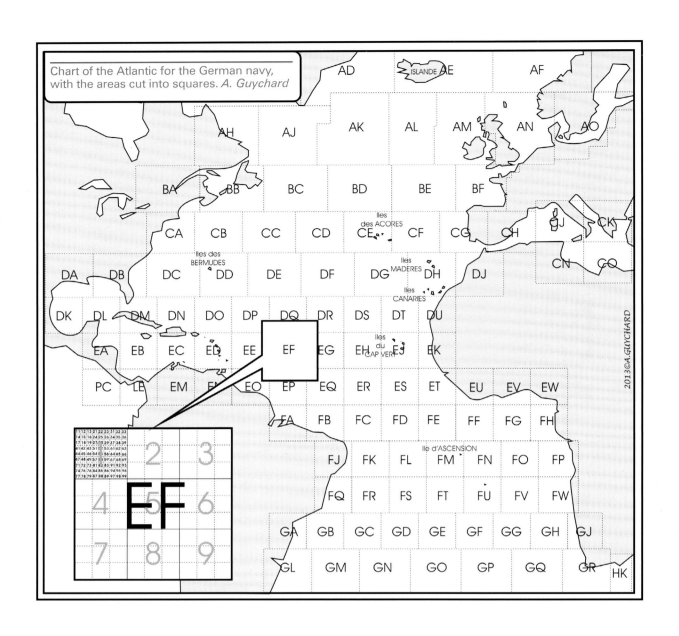

Chart of the Atlantic for the German navy, with the areas cut into squares. *A. Guychard*

Leaving Kiel: on the right is the Laboe Naval Memorial for sailors lost at sea during World War I. *UBA*

The British freighter *Benlawers*, sunk on October 6, was U-123's first success. *DR*

On October 18, U-123 heads toward the SC-7 convoy; it will sink four of the convoy's ships the following day. *UBA*

At 1803 on October 18, the U-boat dives to attack while submerged. *DR*

Convoy Spotted!

At 1600 on October 17, the commander decided to move closer to the English coast, where a convoy had been reported by U-48. At the same time on the following day, a large isolated ship was discovered in the AM 2913 square, close to the British coast. Listening to the traffic radio, Moehle learned that the ship was waiting for a convoy to leave with it. For the moment, the ship advanced slowly in zigzags. At 2021, night fell and the ship stopped. The commander immediately decided to fire a torpedo at a distance of 1,100 meters, which hit the ship and exploded. Since the ship was estimated to weigh 11,400 tons, a second torpedo was fired seven minutes later; it hit its target, but the ship seemed to maintain good buoyancy. At 2030, U-123 surfaced, and at the same time, 300 meters away, the conning tower of another U-boat broke the surface: this was U-99, commanded by Otto Kretschmer. This latter commander sent a lamplight message saying that he was furious to have waited five minutes too long to sink the ship himself. At 2046 a third torpedo was fired by U-123 at the ship, which hadn't started to list, and it finally seemed to sink. This was the 5,458-ton British freighter *Shekatika*, carrying a cargo of 6,000 tons of pit props and 2,003 tons of steel. Suddenly at 2143, flares were fired to port—an entire convoy appeared. U-123 abandoned its first target for the new ones. At 2244 it fired three torpedoes at three freighters at a distance of 2,000 meters, but they changed course and the torpedoes missed them. While it was maneuvering, there was the sound of an explosion—it was a torpedo fired from another U-boat. The ships in the convoy seemed disoriented by all these attacks. At 2320, at a distance of only 800 meters, U-123 fired another torpedo at a steamer estimated as weighing 5,000 tons, but the ship suddenly tacked and the torpedo missed it. Suddenly two escort ships appeared only 300 meters away, and the U-boat moved away at top speed. The convoy was being attacked on all sides, and the ships fled in all directions in a disorderly manner. At 0021 on October 19, Cmdr. Moehle returned to the attack; a torpedo was fired at a freighter estimated as weighing 6,000 tons, but without success, and the ship continued on its way. The shapes of two merchant ships were spotted, along with two escort ships. At 0131, a torpedo was fired at one of the ships, estimated as weighing 7,000 tons; it sank in four minutes. This was the 2,118-ton Dutch freighter *Boekelo*, carrying wood and already damaged by U-100, commanded by Joachim Schepke, two hours earlier. A new target was missed by a torpedo fired at 0135; the second, fired twenty minutes later, hit the machine room of another ship, which sank in five minutes. This was the 5,556-ton British freighter *Sedgepool*, carrying wheat. At 0244, the watch discovered the shape of another freighter that had stopped. At 0317, U-123 approached and fired its last torpedo at a distance of 600 meters. The ship was hit in the middle; it listed to one side and sank in thirty minutes. The commander believed that he had just sunk the sixth ship of his patrol, but in reality it was the freighter *Shekatika*, the ship he had already fired three torpedoes at the night before. This ship was very solid, since it had also resisted a fourth torpedo fired at it by U-100 in the meantime; it had been abandoned by its thirty-six crew members, all of whom had been rescued.

The German personnel based in Lorient welcome Cmdr. Moehle to his new home base. U-123 leaves for maintenance and goes into the arsenal's dock between October 28 and November 4. *LB*

A Freighter Sunk by Gunfire

Since there were no more torpedoes onboard, Karl-Heinz Moehle decided to head directly for Lorient, his new home port. However, at 0435 a merchant ship was spotted. Approaching, the watch could see that it was a freighter loaded with wood and with the aft of the ship partially submerged. It must have been torpedoed in the afternoon and had managed to stay afloat due to its cargo. In spite of the presence of some escort ships not far off, the commander decided to sink it with the gun. After thirty minutes of fire from the 105 mm gun, the 3,106-ton freighter *Clintonia* (the name had been spotted by the U-boat's spotlight) sank. U-123 had just participated in what the German U-boats

nicknamed "the Night of the Long Knives" from October 18 to 20, 1940, which was to be the worst in the war for the British. The convoy SC-7 had the unhappy privilege to be the first target of a really successful wolfpack attack. Spotted by U-48 on October 17, it had also been attacked by U-46, commanded by Endrass; U-99, commanded by Kretschmer; U-100, commanded by Schepke; and U-101, commanded by Mengersen. The convoy lost twenty-one ships, and two others were damaged. The slaughter continued during the nights of October 19 and 20 with the hunting of the HX-79 convoy, which lost twelve freighters. In the morning of October 19, U-123, out of torpedoes, resumed its return to Lorient, sailing at an average of 250 miles a day; the journey was disturbed only twice by the appearance of a plane during the afternoon of October 21. Its new base, the home of the 2nd U-boat Flotilla, was reached at 1125 on October 23.

U-123 arrives in Lorient on October 23, 1940, with a real result of six ships sunk for 25,878 tons. Dönitz has come to congratulate the fifty crew members. *UBA*

Night Attack on the Surface

After a test dive and having its hull demagnetized, U-123 put out of Lorient at 1700 on November 14. On November 17, leaving the Bay of Biscay in the middle of the night, a cry suddenly rang out of the conning tower: "*Mann über Bord*" ("Man overboard"). Due to a particularly heavy wave, the safety belt attached to mechanic Fritz Pfieffer and seaman Werner Bölle had snapped, and the former was swept overboard. The search was abandoned at 0350; it was thought that with his complete leather equipment and boots, he wouldn't have been able to survive more than ten minutes in the freezing water. The mission continued toward the west. At 2357 on November 21, after several days sailing, the watch spotted a steamer in the AL 6572 square. The commander decided on a night attack on the surface, and the crew members got ready at their battle stations. The freighter was estimated as weighing 4,500 tons, heavily loaded, sailing at seven knots. At 0021 on November 10, a torpedo was fired from tube no. 1 at a distance of 1,000 meters: it hit the freighter in the middle. Two lifeboats were lowered, but in spite of this, none of the forty-five crew members were found: a sad fate shared by numerous castaways in the North Atlantic. The ship sank in ten minutes, after sending an SOS by radio: "sss cree 5438n 1853w ar. *Cree* torpedoed sinking fast sss." By looking through the register of commercial ships, the commander found that this was the 4,791-ton British freighter *Cree*; out of Freetown, it was carrying 5,500 tons of iron bars to England.

The conning tower had been painted in camouflage colors before U-123's departure on November 14, 1940. *UBA*

In the middle of the night on November 17, a crew member fell overboard and was lost. In the logbook the commander notes that with all the reservoirs full, the U-boat's buoyancy is very bad; all the big waves go over the conning tower. *UBA*

Life jackets are worn on deck in case of slipping and falling overboard. *From left to right*: Max Hufnagel, commander-in-training Theodor Fahr, and Walter Kaeding. *UBA*

The 5,228-ton British freighter *Tymeric* is torpedoed by U-123 at 0815. *DR*

Convoy!

At four in the morning of November 23, the sea was calmer and a heavily loaded ship was spotted; with a length of 130 meters, it was estimated to weigh 6,000 tons. At 0416 a torpedo was fired from tube 2, and it exploded under the bridge. The ship sank in six minutes, so fast that there were only six survivors out of forty-one. This was the 5,407-ton British freighter *Oakcrest*, which was sailing empty from Liverpool to New York and had lost its convoy OB-244. At 0530 the rest of the convoy came into sight, and onboard everyone got into battle position. It was composed of three columns of ten ships, and for the moment no escort was in sight. At 0551, two torpedoes were fired at freighters estimated as weighing 5,000 to 6,000 tons, then a third two minutes later at a fuel tanker estimated at 8,000 tons. All missed their targets, but the third finally exploded against a ship that was probably in the third column. No one saw the explosion, but they all heard it; according to the Allied radio messages picked up, the commander believed that this was the British freighter *Blairesk*, but no loss was confirmed on the Allies' side. According to the calculations of the length of the torpedo's trajectory, which took two minutes and forty seconds to explode, the ship was at a distance of 2,400 meters. At 0650, a fourth torpedo was fired at a freighter at a distance of only 1,000 meters, but it missed its target. At 0815, another hit the 5,228-ton British freighter *Tymeric*, only 480 meters away. The U-boat, fired at by the artillery of a neighboring ship, couldn't watch its prey sinking, but the ship, carrying 6,150 tons of coal, sank in sixteen minutes; this was the third of U-123's victims that morning. At 0914 the U-boat fired another torpedo at a freighter estimated at 4,000 tons, situated at 800 meters. It exploded in the center of the ship. This fourth ship sunk during that morning was the 5,135-ton Swedish freighter *Anten*, sailing with ballast.

On October 18 the convoy is spotted; during the morning, U-123 sinks four ships. *UBA*

Hit by a Wrecked Ship While Diving

At 0944, as U-123 was still threatened by artillery fire from other ships, it moved away, at the same time reporting the convoy's presence by radio. However, the last ship hit hadn't sunk. To avoid the risk of being aimed at by Allied artillery now that dawn was breaking, the commander decided to sink the ship once and for all by firing a torpedo while submerged. At 1006 the U-boat dived and approached its target by using its electric motors, at a depth of 14 meters. At 1032, when it reached 800 meters, an enormous noise was suddenly heard and a violent shock ran through the U-boat. It had hit something that was floating on the surface, probably the wreck of a damaged ship. The periscope, which was up at the time, was no longer operational. The commander decided to dive to 30 meters to take his boat to safety. At 1938, U-123 surfaced to find considerable damage. The top of the attack periscope had been cut off, the watch periscope was bent backward at an angle of 90 degrees, and the top of the conning tower had been crushed. The commander told his men and then the Befehlshaber der U-Boote (BdU) that they were returning to base. The freighter *Anten* had been abandoned by its crew of thirty-three men, all of whom were safe, and sank forty-eight hours after being torpedoed. At 1430 on November 28, after a five-day journey, U-123 arrived in Lorient.

It is daybreak, and U-123 dives to fire a torpedo while submerged. *UBA*

The U-boat has hit a submerged wreck; the top of its conning tower has been torn off and the periscopes are bent. *UBA*

Passing before Port-Louis Citadel at the entrance to Lorient Port. *UBA*

The coast of Lorient comes into view on November 28; *from left to right*: chief engineer Otto Zschetching, commander-in-training Theodore Fahr, Cmdr. Moehle, IIWO Ernst Cordes, and IWO Johann Jebsen. *UBA*

The crew poses around the commander. Because the damage is very bad, the U-boat will remain in the arsenal for repairs for six weeks. The submariners will have thirteen days of leave in two turns; those who remain behind will help the workers at KNW Lorient with repairs to their boat. *UBA*

U-123 arriving on the Scorff River; we can see the watch periscope bent horizontally. *LB*

Walter Kaeding had this photo taken by a photographer in Lorient as a souvenir of receiving the Iron Cross 2nd Class on December 11. *UBA*

Since the periscopes can't be used, the six victory pennants made onboard during their return journey have been raised on a makeshift mast fixed to the conning tower. *UBA*

Dönitz congratulates the crew; in the foreground is Helmsman Karl Fleige. *UBA*

Commander Moehle recounts his adventure. *From left to right*: Moehle; Herbert "Vati" Schultze, former commander of U-48; Werner Henke, officer aboard U-124; and Joachim Schepke, commander of U-100. The commander will receive the Iron Cross 1st Class, which was awarded to him on October 24. *LB*

Awarding the Iron Cross 2nd Class. The crew will spend Christmas in Carnac and New Year's Eve in Quiberon, two seaside resorts close to Lorient. The IWO, *Oberleutnant zur See* Jebsen, disembarks. Later he will command two U-boats and will die aboard the second on September 23, 1943. *UBA*

Heavy Seas In the North Atlantic

Repaired, U-123 left Lorient at 1800 on January 14, 1941, after an inspection by the chief of the 2nd U-boat Flotilla *Korvettenkapitän* Heinz Fischer. The journey across the Bay of Biscay, nearly all of it on the surface, was interrupted only twice by aerial alerts in the afternoon of January 15. At 1600 five days later, a radio message from U-105 reported a convoy in the AL 6850 square, heading southwest. The weather was still bad and the helmsman had difficulties in situating it precisely. In the morning of January 21, there were no dry deck clothes left, and three men were in their bunks with the flu. In any case, wrote Moehle in the logbook, with the sea at force 4–5 it would be impossible to fire a torpedo at any target. On January 23, the watch couldn't see anything at all. Finally, the following day the weather calmed and a steamer estimated at 6,000 tons was spotted at 1804. U-123 overtook it and waited for nightfall to attack. At 2148, a torpedo was fired from tube 1 at a distance of 600 meters. The ship was hit, its front suddenly rose into the air, and it sank in only fifty seconds. This was the 1,570-ton Norwegian freighter *Vespasian*, lagging behind the convoy OB-276. In the early hours of January 28, U-123 arrived in its new operation zone, the AL 2881 square. In spite of a five-day search toward the south, nothing was sighted, and the radioman just sent in weather reports. At 1945 on February 3, a convoy was reported by U-107 in the AL 0264 square, not far from where U-123 had been six days earlier. The commander gave the order to head there at top speed, 14 knots; he calculated that they could cross its path the next day at midday. At 2339 the radio picked up an SOS from an English ship—it now had the convoy's exact position. Indeed, at 1238 on February 4, a steamer was spotted in the AL 4282 square. At 1539, U-123 dived for a submerged attack; at 1644 it fired a torpedo, which exploded against the ship at a distance of 900 meters. It sank in four minutes; this was the 5,358-ton British freighter *Empire Engineer*, lagging behind the SC-20 convoy and carrying 7,047 tons of steel bars to England. At 1739 the watch saw a shape that quickly turned out to be another German U-boat. Exchanged signals helped them identify U-103, commanded by Schutze, who had been maneuvering into a position to attack the ship when U-123 torpedoed it first. At 2333, everyone was at battle stations. A large isolated ship was spotted to starboard, but as they approached on the surface, the watch identified a fast battle cruiser heading straight for them. The U-boat crash-dived to 65 meters; the large ship passed overhead but didn't drop any depth charges. After waiting for its propeller sounds to fade into the distance, U-123 resurfaced at 0132 on February 5.

Following the accident that had crushed the top of the conning tower, the commander chose an emblem for U-123: the Wound Badge, attributed to the German army's wounded. Indeed, the sailors think of their boat as a living being and not an inert machine, so therefore it should be awarded a decoration as well. *LB*

Crowd gives U-123 a big send-off on January 14, 1941. *UBA*

The newly repaired conning tower and its emblem. The new IWO is *Oberleutnant zur See* Günther Müller-Stockheim. *UBA*

More Defective Torpedoes

Nine monotonous days passed—the ocean was empty in that sector; the radio picked up three SOSs from ships torpedoed elsewhere and continued to send weather reports to the BdU. Suddenly, at 1347 on February 14, a ship weighing 6,000 or 7,000 tons was seen to starboard. The U-boat moved to position itself in front of it for a submerged attack, when, at 1455, another ship came into view, also to starboard. The U-boat immediately dived and approached its new target. At 1536, being at a distance of only 300 meters, it was easily identified as the British *Penolver*, a freighter armed with a gun at the back. U-123 fired a torpedo at it—it didn't work. At 1637 the U-boat was far enough away from the armed ship to surface, but the ship's master was cunning and zigzagged continuously for four hours until nightfall. At 2156, U-123 approached to 4,000 meters and got ready to fire, when the watch saw two large, unmoving shadows to starboard.

Two large freighters. At 2215, Cmdr. Moehle ordered the firing of a first torpedo at the second ship behind the first, estimated as weighing 6,500 tons, at a distance of 1,500 meters. The torpedo cut the surface and was diverted to the left, missing its target. The second torpedo, also set at a depth of 2 meters, was fired at 2224 at the unmoving ship—another miss. The same thing happened with the third torpedo as well as the fourth, set at a depth of 3 meters, while the freighter had resumed its route at 8 knots. The fifth torpedo, fired at 0012 on February 15, was also defective; the sixth, set at a depth of 2 meters and fired at a distance of 1,200 meters, suddenly exploded against the ship, which seemed to be blown into the air, creating a cloud of debris 300 meters high. This was the 6,573-ton British freighter *Alnmoor*, transporting general merchandise made up of flour, steel, and iron alloys out of New York for Glasgow, which had left the SC-21 convoy. Its forty-two crew members were killed in the explosion. Visibility was poor and the other ships weren't found.

After sinking two ships before February 4, the ocean seems empty for nine days. *UBA*

The 6,573-ton British freighter *Alnmoor* was sunk on February 15, 1941. *DR*

3rd Patrol: Four New Successes and the Knight's Cross for Moehle

The Knight's Cross for Commander Moehle

After U-123 having served six days as weather reporter still in the same sector, a message from the BdU relieved it from this task and gave it permission to maneuver as it wished. The commander asked for a report on the fuel stock; since there was only 50 square meters, the maneuvering margin was weak. Moehle decided not to move around too much, to save as much fuel as possible to be able to head toward an eventual convoy reported by radio. As a matter of fact, at 1415 the following day, February 22, a convoy was reported in the AM 2321 square, and the commander decided to head there. At 1010 on February 23, U-96 reported by radio that it had seen the convoy in the AL 3525 square—the U-123 approached still closer. A very big freighter was then spotted by the watch at 1055. In spite of a chase that lasted all afternoon, the merchant ship, which was moving in zigzags at 14 knots, was too fast for the U-boat. The commander, seeing that their fuel level was dropping rapidly, decided to abandon the chase to be able to intervene against the convoy. It was then that the freighter tacked north, putting itself in U-123's path. It was at 2355 when the U-boat, on the surface, fired a first torpedo at it, but it missed its target. A second, fired at 0053 on February 24, exploded in the center of the ship after two minutes and sixteen seconds, a distance of 2,040 meters. A third torpedo was fired at 1,400 meters; even though it broke the surface, it hit its target below the bridge, provoking a great detonation. The ship capsized and sank in twelve minutes; this was the 8,685-ton Dutch freighter *Grootekerk*, transporting general merchandise and coal to Singapore. Because of the low stock of fuel and food, the commander announced to the crew that they were returning to base. U-123 reached Lorient at 1715 on February 28, where a large crowd was waiting to welcome it. *Vizeadmiral* Dönitz was also there, and he personally awarded the decoration of the Knight's Cross to Cmdr. Moehle for having reached the 100,000-ton mark of shipping sunk.

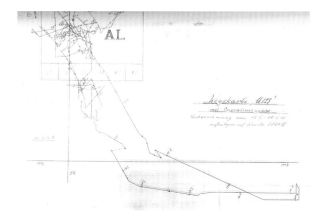

The course taken by U-123 during its third combat patrol: 6,807 miles in forty-six days at sea. *UBA*

The second on the left is No. 1 Seaman Fritz Ufermann; in the center is IIWO Ernst Cordes, who will be leaving the boat for U-103. Later he will command three different U-boats until April 1945 and will survive the war. *UBA*

For awarding the medal, Dönitz stands on the aft deck of U-123, which is moored on the Scorff. *UBA*

The fourth ship sunk by U-123 during this patrol is the 8,685-ton Dutch freighter *Grootekerk*, hit by three torpedoes in the early hours of February 24. *UBA*

U-123 arrives in Lorent on February 28, 1941, with four pennants. The day before, the radio onboard had announced that Cmdr. Moehle had been awarded the Knight's Cross. The tonnage declared destroyed during the third mission was 33,100 tons (in reality, 22,186 tons). *UBA*

The commander has received the Knight's Cross directly from Dönitz. As recorded by war correspondent Kurt Esmarsch, Dönitz congratulates the crew members. *UBA*

Kapitänleutnant Karl-Heinz Moehle, henceforth one of the "Aces." *UBA*

The crew is also awarded Iron Cross 2nd Class medals: on the right is IWO *Oberleutnant zur See* Günther Müller-Stockheim. *UBA*

Nummer 40 SONNABEND, 3. OKTOBER   24. JAHRGANG 1942 Preis 20 Pfennig

Hamburger Illustrierte

„Ihr habt nicht locker gelassen — da
danke ich Euch!" *Der Befehlshaber der Unterseeboote, Admiral Dönitz, bei der V...*
von Auszeichnungen an Männer einer U-Boot-Be...

PK.-Aufnahme Kri...

Their arrival will make the headlines in a German magazine the
following year. *LB*

Vorläufiges Besitzzeugnis

**Der Führer
und Oberste Befehlshaber
der Wehrmacht**

hat

dem Kapitänleutnant Karl-Heinz Moehle

**das Ritterkreuz
des Eisernen Kreuzes**

am 26. Februar 1941 verliehen.

Berlin , den 14. März 1941.

Kapitän zur See und Abt. Chef im MPA.

The certificate confirming Cmdr. Moehle's
medal. *UBA*

The crew is waved off to the sound of the brass band. A Kriegsmarine U-boat chaser based in Lorient escorts U-123 until it is out to sea; a crash dive is specially organized to train the ship. On April 11, in the Bay of Biscay, a second exercise dive will take place as part of the new crew members' training. *LB*

From left to right: No. 2 Seaman Walter Kaeding, Herman Holz, and IWO Muller-Stockheim. *UBA*

A Neutral Freighter Is Sunk outside Its Official Route

At 1800 on April 10, U-123 put out of Lorient for its fourth patrol, heading for the North Atlantic. It advanced on the surface at an average of 220 miles a day. At 2040 on April 15, a radio message was picked up: the BdU gave U-123 an operation sector between the AD 78 and AK 24 squares, between Iceland and Greenland. The U-boat changed course and headed dead north. At 0430 on April 17, in the AK 6791 square, a steamer was spotted sailing 20 miles south of the passage reserved for neutral ships. The decision to pursue it was taken, and the diesel motors were pushed to their maximum. Visibility was excellent, and at 1505 U-123 dived for a submerged attack. At 1550 a torpedo was fired from an aft tube at a distance of 1,160 meters, and it exploded in the center of the ship. The crew members climbed down into lifeboats. The ship was identified as the 6,991-ton Swedish freighter *Venezuela*. A second torpedo was fired at 600 meters, but there was no explosion. A third, set at a depth of 3 meters, was fired at 1603, creating a heavy explosion, and the ship listed 10 degrees. Because it was a large, modern ship, the commander decided to fire a fourth torpedo, which exploded in the machine room; the freighter took on more water but still didn't sink. A fifth torpedo, fired at 800 meters, didn't explode. At 1928 U-123 surfaced, but the sea, at force 4, didn't permit it to use artillery. Finally, the ship sank. In the early hours of April 22, U-123 reached the AD 7998 square between Greenland and Iceland. A radio message sent it to the AL 33 square, west of the British Isles.

Cmdr. Moehle in U-123's conning tower on April 1941, leaving for the fourth patrol. His new IIWO is *Leutnant zur See* Horst von Schroeter. *UBA*

The U-123 Attacked by a Plane

At 1935 on April 27: aerial alert! The U-boat immediately dived, changed course and descended to 60 meters. At 1949, five bombs dropped by the plane exploded, but too far away to do any damage. Between 2030 and 2109, three series of explosions occurred in the distance, about 20 miles away. The commander thought it was maneuvers by a group of bombers with destroyers to keep the U-boat submerged, to give them time to reach its position. Therefore, at 2124, he gave the order to surface and move away to the west at top speed. At 2314 in the AL 5335 square, the watch saw an entire convoy to port, heavily escorted. At 0121 on April 28, the radio onboard reported the convoy heading east. For over an hour U-123 tried to penetrate into the convoy to reach the merchant ships, but each time it was repulsed by an escort ship, probably warned of the German U-boat's presence by the plane the day

before. Its new approach attempts until dawn were equally unsuccessful; the commander decided to keep a distance during the day—an attack would certainly be possible when other U-boats and the Luftwaffe eventually arrived. He waited for U-95, U-96, U-65, and U-552, whose grouped attacks should keep the escort ships busy. On the basis of the observation of smoke, the convoy was made up of three columns of ships. The radio onboard continued to give precise indications about the convoy's itinerary at 0748 and at 1210. The source of the transmission of these two messages had probably been intercepted by the Allies; at 1347 the watch in U-123's conning tower saw two destroyers heading straight for them at an estimated speed of 15 knots. The sea, at force 4–5, made defense impossible. The commander gave the order to move away at top speed toward the west. At 1700 the sea was empty, but any chance of finding the convoy again, which was still heading east at that moment, was now lost.

U-123 resurfaces after diving to avoid a patrol aircraft. *UBA*

Depth-Charged by Destroyers

At 0800 on April 29, in the AL 3246 square, smoke was seen; probably a freighter damaged by U-96, thought the commander. He decided to approach to eventually deliver the coup de grâce. At 1015, the watch saw masts and a chimney rising out of the smoke; they must belong to a large fuel tanker of about 8,000 tons. Suddenly, five minutes later: Alert! Crash-dive! Two destroyers about 3,000 meters behind the smoking wreck appeared; U-123 descended to 130 meters. The submariners anxiously waited for the warships' reactions: it was their first depth-charging since their departure on operations in 1940. The first two charges exploded at 1035 a long way off, but the following twelve, fifteen minutes later, which exploded just above the back of the U-boat, tossed it about heavily. The destroyer was using its location-spotting Asdic system to precisely locate the U-boat. The characteristic echoes, "ping, ping," resounded in the ocean. At 1100 a new series of depth charges exploded just above the conning tower: Was this the end? However, the charges dropped between 1106 and 1116 were farther away. Then, at 1122 and 1208, another two series of five depth charges exploded above the conning tower. In all, the crew members counted about one hundred explosions; some near, others farther away. Then, nothing more; the U-boat escaped by using its electric motors and surfaced at 1955. However, only two minutes later, a new alert and another crash dive—a seaplane flying out of the setting sun. U-123 broke the surface at 2115, and the commander wrote in the logbook: "Finally, fresh air is coming inside again!" The U-boat moved away from this too-dangerous zone; besides, it had received by radio a new operation zone in the AL 23-24 squares. At 1629 on May 1, 1941, in the AL 1492 square, the watch saw smoke on the port horizon. Ten minutes later: Alert! The smoke was coming from a destroyer, which was heading straight for them at top speed. The same scenario that had been played out two days earlier was repeated: descent to 130 meters, the wait, the explosion of the first seven depth charges at 1750, and then the pursuit until 1937. However, this time the charges exploded too far away to put them in any danger. U-123 surfaced at 2230 and received a new patrol sector by radio: the AE 8725 square. However, reaching this zone, the commander gave the order to return to base since the fuel was getting too low. In the hope of crossing a ship or a convoy, the homebound route was done in zigzags, changing course every four hours. It reached Lorient at 0824 on May 11, after thirty-one days at sea and 5,952 miles covered. The command was transferred to *Kapitänleutnant* Reinhard Hardegen on May 19, 1941.

Smoke on the horizon! Approaching on the surface, U-123 discovers two destroyers hidden behind the wreck. *UBA*

The two destroyers drop depth charges to sink U-123, which descends to a depth of 130 meters. The crew members count around 100 explosions. *LB*

This was Cmdr. Moehle's last mission; he had been named chief of the 5th Training Flotilla in Kiel. His total results are twenty-one ships sunk for 93,846 tons, out of which were seventeen ships for 83,599 tons while commander of U-123. To the right is an army officer of the 11th Battalion of the 358th Regiment of the 205th Infantry Division, the patron unit of U-123. *UBA*

Inspected by *Vizeadmiral* Dönitz on May 13, 1940, Cmdr. Moehle, his IWO *Oberleutnant zur See* Müller-Stockheim, and the chief engineer Otto Zschetsching say farewell to the rest of the crew. Gunther Müller-Stockheim will command U-67, with which he will win the Knight's Cross before being killed on July 16, 1943. *UBA*

Return to Lorient on May 11, 1941, this time with only one success. *UBA*

The crew members have been given special tropical equipment, so they know that their next destination won't be the North Atlantic. On June 7, the men load foodstuff into the U-boat; the departure is for the following day at 1841. *DR*

A Portuguese Freighter Sunk by Mistake

After a departure at 1841 on June 8, U-123 had to turn back to Lorient to get repairs done on the hydraulic system for working the periscopes. It left again at 0800 on June 15 and headed south. Two Spanish freighters were seen on June 17 and 19. June 20 was described in a few words in the logbook—nothing to report. This was because the first torpedoing Hardegen carried out as commander of U-123 had been erased from the logbook on the order from Admiral Dönitz—a very rare event! U-123 had sunk a Portuguese freighter (and thus neutral) by mistake. The 4,333-ton freighter *Ganda* was sailing peacefully off Casablanca when it was hit by a first torpedo fired from U-123 at 2010. After the crew had scrambled into lifeboats, the U-boat fired another torpedo nine minutes later and then sank the ship with the gun. It was when they approached the castaways that the commander realized that he had made a mistake. Out of the crew of sixty-six men, five had been killed. This destruction of a neutral ship could have created serious diplomatic repercussions between Portugal and Germany.

The command of U-123 is transferred to Reinhard Hardegen on May 19. This officer belongs to the second generation of commanders trained in peacetime, having acquired experience during the first year of the war as IWO aboard a combat U-boat. He had already been to Lorient twice before aboard U-124 in 1940. *LB*

Hardegen was born in Bremen in 1913, the town where U-123 was built. In his youth he sailed a lot and passed his pilot's license before joining the U-boat Corps. He was twenty-eight years old when he took command of U-123. *LB*

For its fifth combat patrol the conning tower has been painted with striped camouflage. A 37 mm gun has been mounted on the aft deck. The new IWO is *Oberleutnant zur See* Herbert Schneider, and the new LI is Heinz-Walter Schulz. In the background is U-201. *Charita*

Firing the gun at the Portuguese freighter *Ganda* on June 20, 1941. *DR*

Calculating the itinerary with the charts in the control room. *DR*

Secret Resupplying in a Canary Island Port

The U-123 continued south. On June 22, the watch admired the mountainous Portuguese islands of Porto Santo and then Madeira to port. Onboard, everyone was stupefied: the radio connected to the loudspeakers retransmitted the news from the Wehrmacht High Command announcing that Germany had declared war on the USSR. In the logbook, Cmdr. Hardegen noted that the news was a real bombshell; no one had been expecting this to happen. At 1340, a radio message from the BdU reported that U-123 should go to receive supplies in the Canary Isles in the night of June 24–25 from the ship *Corrientes*, which was hiding under the name of *Culebra*. At 0200 on June 25, the U-boat observed fishing boats entering and leaving Gran Canaria Port. When traffic calmed down, it slipped in behind a fishing boat and entered the port. At 0356, it berthed alongside *Culebra*, where the supplies had been perfectly prepared. Boxes of food were transferred to the U-boat in total silence, along with fuel. At 0640, U-123 put out to sea, ready to head for the distant sector, where the Allies wouldn't be expecting it. At 0310 on June 27, U-69 reported by radio a convoy in the DT 6220 square off the coast of Mauritania. Hardegen decided to go and intercept this convoy, and he calculated his plan.

Inside the Convoy

At 1159, the convoy was in sight—seven columns of smoke. However, when the U-boat approached on the surface, a plane appeared, probably a Sunderland, which forced it to dive to 20 meters. U-123 rose to periscope depth—the seaplane was still there at a distance of 4,000 meters. After two hours, the U-boat resurfaced and advanced at top speed to try to find the convoy again, which it did at 1634. However, the seaplane was still there, as well as two destroyers acting as escorts. The convoy was composed of four columns of freighters, spaced at about 1,200 meters and protected by escort ships on each side. The U-boat had to wait until nightfall to penetrate the column from behind between two columns. At 2357, 2358, and midnight, three torpedoes were fired in the respective direction of a 10,000-ton fuel tanker, a 6,000-ton freighter, and an 8,000-ton fuel tanker. After two explosions the last tanker that was aimed at tacked to port, and the torpedo intended for it exploded after two minutes and fifty-eight seconds against a ship farther away in the convoy; although this destruction was heard, it wasn't seen and was never confirmed by the Allies. The first ship to sink was the 5,646-ton British freighter *P.L.M.22*, hit in the middle, which was carrying 7,600 tons of iron bars. The second, also hit in the middle, was the 1,996-ton Dutch freighter *Oberon*. The two ships were part of the SL-78 convoy on a Douala-Freetown-Hull route. While U-123 escaped on the surface by the tail end of the convoy, it came under artillery fire from a steamer and was spotted by a corvette, which was on the port side of the convoy and headed straight for the U-boat after launching a lit-up buoy. At 0014 on June 28, the U-boat dived and descended to 65 meters. The corvette dropped depth charges in series of six, which exploded in the right direction but too far above the submersible. The corvette didn't appear to be equipped with Asdic; the U-boats counted thirty-three explosions before things calmed down. At 0215, U-123 resurfaced and the radioman sent his report to the BdU. The convoy came into sight again at 0527, but it was too late for a new attack with dawn breaking. At 0719, a destroyer headed toward it, and the U-boat crash-dived, but there were no repercussions. Cmdr. Hardegen thought that perhaps the destroyer wanted to keep them underwater to allow the convoy to continue on a slanting course toward the north. When they resurfaced at 0826 the ocean was empty. A new course was set at 320 degrees, and the convoy came back into sight at 0920. At 1014 the seaplane appeared and the submersible immediately dived to 20 meters. Six minutes later, four depth charges exploded above the U-boat, which was tossed about, and the glass on the depth gauge shattered. The commander was surprised by the bombs' precision; he thought that the plane had spotted the location where they had dived, due to the calm sea. The U-boat descended to 40 meters, and at 1030 two more bombs exploded far away. At 1124 eleven depth charges exploded and the sound of a destroyer's propellers could be heard. The U-boat descended to 65 meters. Until 1215, the crew counted fifty-three depth charges, the first well placed and then farther off; the last were surprisingly close, but the U-boat sustained no damage. U-123 surfaced at 1556 to find an empty sea; the commander decided to head north to find the convoy again, effecting regular changes of course toward the west.

Two freighters were sunk during the night of June 27–28. *DR*

On June 28 U-123 is depth-charged several times by a corvette; it dives to 65 meters. *LB*

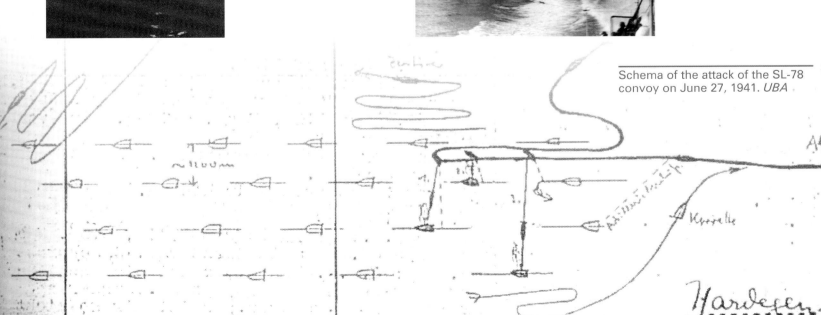

Schema of the attack of the SL-78 convoy on June 27, 1941. *UBA*

A U-boat Trap?

At 0705 on June 29, the Sunderland was spotted, which made Hardegen think that the convoy was indeed northwest of their position, and effectively it was found at 1142. When they approached, the commander saw an isolated ship sailing in zigzags to port of the convoy; was it an escort ship or a U-boat trap? At 1831, he decided to approach it and dived; at 1936 a torpedo was fired at the target, which was at a distance of only 350 meters, causing a huge explosion. The commander wrote in the logbook, "Armed merchantman *Rio Azul*, 4,088 tons." The freighter broke in two and sank in just over two minutes; it was carrying 6,700 tons of iron. At 1940, U-123 surfaced and found itself in a sea full of debris. The convoy was now a long way away; Hardegen noted that the sunken freighter had paid the price for keeping its distance from it. At 2100 on June 30, the radioman reported to the BdU that the convoy had been lost for over thirty-three hours; he asked for permission to continue the mission toward the south. At 0845 the following day, he received an affirmative reply.

After losing the convoy, U-123 continues south on July 1. Cmdr. Hardegen and Dr. Gerhard Petzold relax against the rail. *UBA*

The 5,444-ton British freighter *Auditor* was sunk on July 4, 1941. *DR*

The shark is hoisted in front of the 105 mm gun. The officer in white is IIWO Horst von Schroeter. *UBA*

On July 27 a shark is caught. *UBA*

Crossing the equator on July 27. The entire afternoon is given over to a sportive party on the U-boat's foredeck, with a sack race, a tug of war, and trying to catch sausages suspended from the antenna wire. And handing out prizes at the end. *UBA*

Sack race. The shark's fins have been attached to the antenna cable. *UBA*

A Freighter Sunk with Ten Planes Onboard!

U-123 continued its route west of the Canaries and then arrived 600 miles northwest of the Cape Verde Islands. At 1658 on July 3, the watch spotted smoke to starboard. The U-boat approached on the surface and found that it belonged to an isolated freighter of about 5,500 tons, with two masts and a chimney stack; the ship was sailing in unending zigzags. At 1939 the U-boat dived, but, although it was only 1,100 meters from its target, it couldn't fire a torpedo because the ship was constantly changing course. Finally it surfaced at 2129, but the moon was too bright for the moment. At 0245 on July 4, the moon had disappeared and everyone was at battle stations aboard the U-boat. U-123 moved up to the ship on a parallel course of 2,000 meters at about 12 knots to overtake it and position itself in the ship's path. At 0355 a torpedo was fired at a distance of 1,000 meters, and it exploded after sixty-three seconds. The sinking ship sent out an SOS on the 600-meter band: "SSS, Auditor g k m j, 25.47N,

28.25W torpedo." Two lifeboats were lowered, and after twenty-three minutes the freighter had disappeared. This was the 5,300-ton British merchant ship *Auditor*, which was carrying 5,300 tons of diverse merchandise and ten planes from Liverpool to Table Bay and then Beira; only one man out of the seventy-six crew members was lost. U-123 now headed for the African coast, six days of sailing alone on the ocean. Reaching the coast, the U-boat descended south and reached the ET 2671 square at 1600 on July 17. It was now thirteen days since it had last fired a torpedo. Off Freetown during the next two days, three freighters were seen, but they were sailing under the American flag. In addition, the approach to the port was guarded by two warships. Hardegen decided to change the operation sector, head west, and then turn toward the Cape Verde Islands. On July 20, the sudden appearance of a plane forced the U-boat to crash-dive. On July 27 in the EH 9751 square, all the motors were stopped and a party was held onboard to celebrate crossing the equator. At 2000, seeing that the fuel stock had descended to 80 square meters and informed by the BdU that receiving more wasn't possible, the commander announced the return to Lorient.

Tug of war. Since their surface resupply boats had been sunk by the Royal Navy in June, several U-boats operating in the South Atlantic, such as U-123, were forced to return to their base. *UBA*

Convoy toward Gibraltar

From 2000 to 2339 on July 30, four torpedoes stocked under the deck were transferred inside the U-boat. On August 7, with a fuel stock of 35 square meters, the commander decided to slant to the northeast to get closer to Gibraltar, where he had heard that a convoy was expected. On August 12, a message from U-93, U-94, and U-331 reported that the convoy was close to his current position, and a German Fw 200 Condor aircraft reconfirmed its exact position at 1820. Hardegen estimated that he would cross the convoy at 2200 in the CG 4556 square. At 2030 a detonation was heard to port. At 2127 smoke from freighters was spotted, and then a destroyer, which was headed in their direction—it must be at the head of the convoy. At 2230, the destroyer had tacked; the watch discovered a U-boat on the surface—the U-126—and lamp signals were exchanged. The destroyer had passed them; it shouldn't be long before they saw the merchant ships in the convoy. A Condor flew over them at 1612, and a second at 1615. At 1717, a Condor dropped a bomb that the watch saw on the horizon, and then it flew toward them. Using a spotlight, it signaled that the convoy was to be found in the direction of 180 degrees. U-123 advanced but found only a destroyer in the distance. But the Condor flew back over the U-boat without realizing that it was giving away their position. As the commander expected, the destroyer headed directly toward them, and at 1735 they crash-dived to 65 meters and changed course 270 degrees by using the electric motors, before slowing down ten minutes later. After an hour, nothing had been heard and the commander thought that the destroyer had returned to the convoy, and he decided to rise to 20 meters. All of a sudden the destroyer's Asdic sound was heard, and the U-boat immediately dived to 60 meters. It had just reached this depth when the first series of depth charges exploded close by. The U-boat sailed at a depth between 75 and 85 meters. The hydrophone detected two destroyers, which, in seven attacks, dropped a series of three depth charges six times. In all, the crew counted 126 explosions, thirty-nine of which were very close. Everything aboard was thrown about, but the technical crew kept its calm and repaired the damage between each series of explosions. The last depth charges were heard at 2150, the last Asdic sounds at 2230. The commander decided to resurface in the dark at 0005 on August 14. After nine days sailing north, U-123 reached Lorient at 0910 on August 23, 1941.

On August 24, 1941, U-126 arrives in Lorient. In the foreground we can see the back of U-123's conning tower, with its pennants showing the tonnage of the six ships reported sunk, notably the 5,444-ton British freighter *Auditor*, sunk on July 4, and the 4,333-ton Portuguese freighter *Ganda*, sunk on June 20. *UBA*

Return to Lorient on August 23, 1941. Major Kammerer, chief of U-123's patron battalion and female army transmissions auxiliaries, chats with Hardegen, who will receive the Iron Cross 1st Class the same day. During its fifth combat patrol, U-123 covered 12,404 miles, of which only 151 miles were while submerged. *UBA*

A buoy attached to a raft is fished out of the water. It will be offered to the patron battalion and will be hung over the chimney in the officer's mess. *DR*

From left to right, with a female auxiliary: Helmsman Wilhelm Schiffer (the patron battalion's warrant officer), Horst von Schroeter, and *OMasch* Karl Latislaus. Maintenance work will last six weeks, and the men will spend their R&R in two turns in Carnac. *UBA*

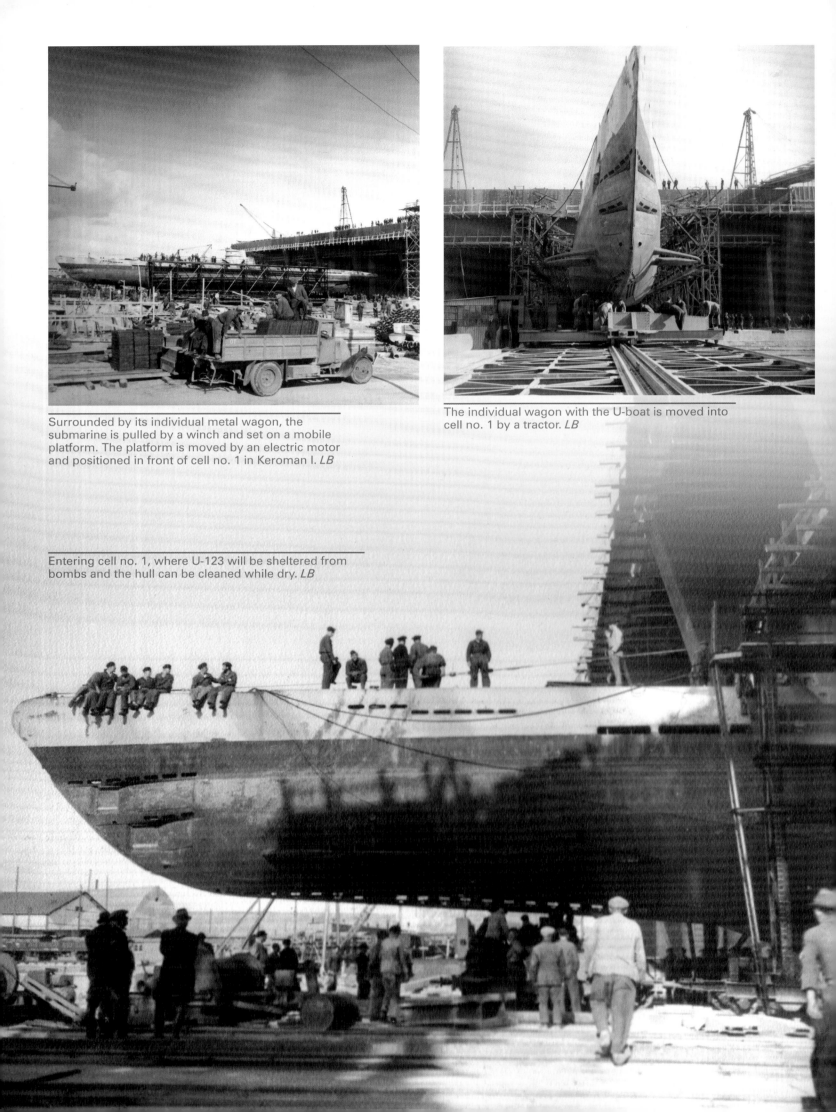

Surrounded by its individual metal wagon, the submarine is pulled by a winch and set on a mobile platform. The platform is moved by an electric motor and positioned in front of cell no. 1 in Keroman I. *LB*

The individual wagon with the U-boat is moved into cell no. 1 by a tractor. *LB*

Entering cell no. 1, where U-123 will be sheltered from bombs and the hull can be cleaned while dry. *LB*

A Castaway Is Taken Aboard

On October 14 1941, U-123 put out of Lorient and headed west. At 0400 on October 20, a radio message from the BdU affected it to the Schlagetot wolfpack. It was to take the position of reconnaissance in the AJ square off Canada, but at 1650, a radio message from U-84 reported a convoy in the BE 1556 square, which was much closer. U-123 set a course northeast, planning to reach the convoy between 0200 and 0400 the following day. Indeed, at 0346 on October 21, the watch spotted four large silhouettes of ships to starboard. Approaching on the surface, they could see four freighters weighing between 10,000 and 15,000 tons, protected by three destroyers, all sailing at high speed. There was no time to lose: at 0428, as a destroyer was approaching in its direction, U-123 fired three torpedoes in the direction of the largest freighter, at a distance of 1,500 meters. Two explosions were heard after eighty-one seconds. Now for the others: The pursuit lasted over an hour, but since they were sailing at about 15 knots and continually changing course, the U-boat couldn't overtake them to get into firing position. At 0614, a destroyer turned in its direction, and it had to move away. Finally, the U-boat returned to the

place where the torpedoing had taken place, and at 1009 discovered large pools of oil, debris, and a lone man in a lifeboat. The castaway was taken aboard, and he told them that his ship was the 13,984-ton British armed merchant cruiser HMS *Aurania*. It had been hit by one torpedo in the back and by another under the bridge in the turbine room. Most of the 250 men onboard would have been saved by one of the destroyers. The survivor had heard the sounds of the ship sinking. The radio aboard reported the destruction of *Aurania* and received a "Bravo" reply almost immediately. The truth was completely different. After being torpedoed, the ship listed 25 degrees and a lifeboat carrying six men was lowered too quickly. The lifeboat capsized when it hit the water, and three men were picked up later by a destroyer, while the three others were finally reported as missing. The master of *Aurania* managed to right his ship to a list of only 15 degrees and left the sector at a speed of 8 knots, while U-123 was chasing after the other ships. Of the three men reported missing, only one had survived by clinging to the capsized lifeboat. This man was Bertie Shaw, taken aboard the U-boat as a prisoner for the rest of the patrol. The badly damaged armed merchant cruiser managed to reach a port in England and, after nineteen months of repair, put out to sea once more.

A convoy is reported by radio on October 20, and Hardegen takes stock on the chart with his IWO *Oberleutnant zur See* Herbert Schneider. *DR*

Cmdr. Hardegen in Paris between two patrols. *LB*

Several of U-123's crew members, mixing with an army unit in front of the Tomb of the Unknown Soldier under the Arc de Triomphe in Paris. *LB*

Attacked by a Seaplane and a Light Cruiser

During the afternoon of October 21 the U-boat had to dive twice following the appearance of a seaplane at 1325 and at 1529. At 1605, after a quick glance through the periscope and seeing that the horizon and the sea appeared to be empty, Hardegen decided to surface. He later gave this account: "Suddenly, an image appeared that until then we had only ever seen in the film *U-Boote Westwärts*. Well, we had all seen the movie aboard. At first I thought I was hallucinating. In front of me, at a distance of only 3 miles, was a huge convoy. Wide eyed, I counted twenty-two large steamers and three destroyers. I hadn't seen anything through the periscope due to the force 3–4 sea. Ten minutes [earlier] and we would have surfaced right in the middle of it! Since I had obviously been spotted, my first thought was to stay on the surface and report the convoy. As we moved away, the radio transmitted its position and described the number of ships and escorts, their speed, and their direction. Not only did a destroyer approach, the seaplane suddenly reappeared! At 1707 we crash-dived, and when we reached a depth of 25 meters two bombs exploded, the first above the deck, the second above the front. Although it was tossed about, the U-boat remained waterproof and descended to 80 meters. The destroyer passed above us twice but didn't drop any depth charges; it had turned on its search apparatus. I decided to wait for dark before resurfacing at 2210. We heard the detonation of two torpedoes in the distance: our action had therefore been of use to other U-boats." In spite of searching for several hours, the convoy wasn't to be found. At 1550 on October 22, a U-boat came into view. It was U-82, which told them that the convoy should be found at 180 degrees. Then, at 2310, a radio message from U-203 specified the exact position of the convoy, and Hardegen thought he would be able to find it in the next three hours. However, at the same time an oil leak was discovered; a reservoir had probably been damaged by the bombs from the plane. At 0119 on October 23, a red light was seen to starboard for about thirty seconds. The sea was heavy and the conning tower was regularly covered by waves, which made observation difficult. Suddenly, at 0143, a silhouette appeared to starboard. The commander recounted: "A warship passed us at only 1,500 meters away. It was too big to be a destroyer. It had two chimney stacks behind the DCA posts that were just as high. Probably a small D- or C-class cruiser. From its parallel course it tacked 80 degrees; all the tubes were ready. It appeared not to have seen us, but suddenly it tacked right toward us. It was so close—goodbye convoy! Crash-dive! When we were 40 meters a first series of seven depth charges exploded some way off, and we descended to 85 meters. On the basis of the slow, dull propeller sounds, it was indeed a light cruiser. Its search apparatus made a different sound than the Asdic: a regular sch-sch. We counted four series of seven depth charges. Everything was thrown about inside the U-boat, which filled with 10 tons of water. I would have to resurface as soon as possible to take advantage of full dark to be able to escape before a group of U-boat hunters found us. Our prisoner didn't seem to appreciate our situation and kept muttering to himself, 'No good, no good!' At 0430 there was a last series of explosions and then no more sounds from the search apparatus." At 0522, U-123 surfaced and escaped silently, first using its electric motors for half an hour and then its diesel motors at full speed.

Last instant of sun before getting far out to sea. *LB*

The 13,984-ton British armed merchant cruiser *Aurania* is damaged by a torpedo fired from U-123; the crew believes that it has sunk. *DR*

U-123 leaves Lorient on October 14, 1941. Ship traffic in the South isn't heavy; would targets be more numerous in the North Atlantic? *LB*

When U-123 surfaced the second time, the watchmen discovered an entire convoy only 3 miles away, which had not been seen at periscope depth because of the swells. *LB*

Wolfpack Attack Hindered by Fog

After sailing west for four days, the oil leak having been repaired, the AJ 5512 square was reached at midday on October 30. This was the reconnaissance position fixed by the BdU within the Schlagetot wolfpack. At 1240, a new radio message from the BdU sent it to a new sector: the AH 9820 square, which signified the Strait of Belle Isle, between the Canadian coast and Newfoundland Island. Between 1610 and 1735 on November 1, several radio messages from different U-boats reported convoys, one of which was easily attainable. The commander wrote in the logbook: "Farewell old lighthouses of Belle Isle. Today alone, five different convoys are surrounded. The gray wolves have multiplied." At

1710 in the BC 1257 square on November 2, after sailing southeast the previous day, the watch spotted the freighters. Hardegen wrote that cooperation had worked out well. Since it was still light, U-123 kept its distance. At 1930, U-38 appeared; by nightfall U-82, U-202, and U-569 had the convoy in sight. There were only four boats missing from the new Raubritter wolfpack, which should be arriving any time now, and Hardegen had decided to wait until they were all there before attacking. However, at 0103 on November 3, the detonation of a torpedo was heard, as well as at 0206 and 0217. Several U-boat conning towers were seen in the direction of the convoy. At 0400, the commander decided to approach the convoy on the surface and then attack underwater. Between 0457 and 0537, a total of eight torpedo detonations were heard. But suddenly, the

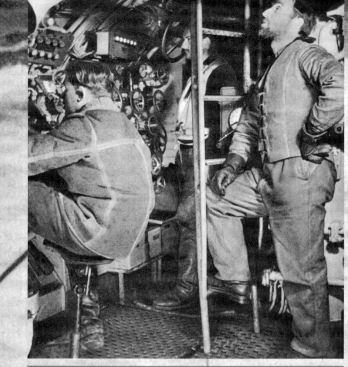

Preparing for a submerged attack on November 3. The chief engineer tells the commander at the periscope in the conning tower the depth to the seabed. *DR*

moon was hidden by fog; it was too dark for a submerged attack and too light for a surface attack. Hardegen decided to wait until the moon set and the sun rose, and alongside, U-203 seemed to be doing the same. But toward 0745, the fog lifted and the horizon grew lighter: it was the moment. At 0806, U-123 headed directly for the convoy. Hardegen could make out several silhouettes finally disappearing into the fog. He recounted: "Just as the U-boat prepared to attack, the detonation of a torpedo close by tossed everything aboard about. However, we couldn't see anything. It must have been U-203 that had fired. Then another silhouette, but this time the bow was to starboard. Either it was another column of ships or they had tacked west. We could barely make out three large steamers; beside them were a destroyer and a corvette keeping an active watch on the sector. Two torpedoes were fired at a distance of 1,500 meters in the direction of freighters estimated as weighing 7,000 tons, but they didn't explode. The targets had already disappeared into the fog, but the corvette appeared to have seen us and headed straight for us. I decided to leave the zone." At 0849 and at 0883 two more torpedo detonations were heard. At 0932 the SC52 convoy was once again in view, but the U-boat had to leave again following the appearance of a destroyer that was heading straight for it. With the daylight, a surface attack was now impossible. U-123 headed north but spent five days surrounded by fog. On November 11, with a fuel stock of 35 square meters, Hardegen announced their return to base to the crew. Lorient was reached at 1000 on November 22, after forty days at sea. The U-boat had covered 6,666 miles, 88 of them while submerged. The prisoner, Bertie Shaw, was disembarked on arrival.

In the afternoon of October 21, U-123, on the surface, is forced to dive twice following the appearance of a seaplane. *DR*

Between 0204 and 0430 on October 23, the crew members anxiously listen to the explosions caused by depth charges dropped at them by a light cruiser. *DR*

Watch duties on October 30 in the AJ 5512 square, south of Greenland and east of Canada. *DR*

After five days of fog, U-123 turns homeward on November 11. *DR*

To determine how to reach the reported convoy, the commander studies the chart in the control room. *DR*

U-123 returns from its mission on November 22, 1941, with a red pennant for HMS *Aurania*, which the crew members mistakenly believe they have sunk, according to the account given by one of the ship's crew, Bertie Shaw, taken aboard and brought to Lorient. IWO Herbert Schneider is disembarked; he will take command of U-522, aboard which he will win the Knight's Cross a month before being killed on January 16, 1943. *UBA*

First Ship Sunk during Operation Drumbeat

After the Japanese attacked Pearl Harbor on December 7, 1941, the Germans and the Italians declared war on the United States four days later. Because all the restrictions concerning American ships had been lifted, Dönitz prepared Operation "Paukenschlag" (Drumbeat) off the coast of the United States. U-123 was one of the five U-boats chosen to take part in the first wave of attack, and it left Lorient on December 23. The next day, to celebrate Christmas peacefully in the dangerous Bay of Biscay, the U-boat dived and remained underwater between 1200 and 1900. It crossed the North Atlantic without incident, covering an average of 150 miles a day to economize on fuel. At midnight on January 9, a radio message from the BdU ordered U-123 to position itself off New York. Approaching and listening to the open radio on the 600-meter-frequency band, a lot of interesting details were learned, notably the ports where freighters were expected. However, the U-boat had to wait for the other U-boats to get into position to launch an attack together at the same time—the "drumbeat that Dönitz wanted," unless it spotted a target weighing over 10,000 tons. As it happened, at 1635 on January 11, 125 miles southeast of Cape Sable, the watch spotted at freighter with two tall masts and a taller chimney stack; with these characteristics, it could belong only to the Blue Funnel Line, weighing a tonnage equal to that fixed by the admiral. At 0149 on January 12, after approaching, U-123 fired a torpedo that exploded after ninety seconds. Even though it was shipping water through the bows and the lifeboats had been lowered, it didn't sink. Its radio messages identified it as the 9,076-ton British freighter *Cyclops*. At 0218, U-123 fired a second torpedo, which caused a heavy explosion; the ship broke in two and sank in five minutes. This was the first ship to be sunk in American waters since Pearl Harbor.

The patron battalion arrives with Christmas trees before U-123 leaves on December 23, 1941. *UBA*

A discussion in Lorient in mid-December 1941. *From left to right*: Ernst Kals, commander of U-130; Heinrich Bleichrodt, commander of U-109; Ulrich Folkers, of U-125; and Reinhard Hardegen. The four of them will be the first to sail to the US—only Richard Zapp of U-66 is missing. *LB*

Sailing toward the high seas in the wake of a minesweeper. *UBA*

The trees are installed on the top of the conning tower before the departure. *UBA*

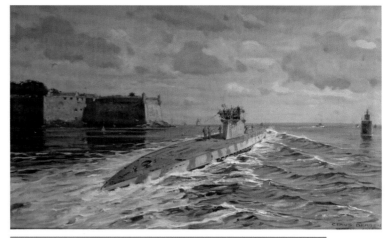

Painting of U-123 departing Lorient on December 23, with the old fort at left. *UBA*

Chef Hannes Vonderschen prepares Christmas cakes. *DR*

U-123 dives in the afternoon of December 24 to celebrate Christmas. *From left to right*: the new IWO Hoffmann; the commander, IIWO Schroeter; and LI Heinz-Walter Schulz. *UBA*

Christmas carols accompanied by an accordion—for a few hours the war is forgotten. At midnight on December 31, Cmdr. Hardegen writes in the logbook: "A new year starts in the North Atlantic. The crew can look back on our last successful year and confidently turn toward the new one, which will contribute toward the end of the war." *DR*

The British freighter *Cyclops*, sunk on January 12, 1942, is the first ship destroyed during Operation Paukenschlag and the twenty-fifth by U-123, notes Hardegen. It is also, following Pearl Harbor, the first ship sunk by enemy action in American waters. *DR*

U-123's mission off New York has made the headlines in the German newspapers. Hardegen, while a sea cadet aboard the light cruiser *Karlsruhe*, had visited the town in 1934. *LB*

One of the eight ships sunk by U-123 during this mission, torpedoed in the middle of the night. *DR*

Five Torpedoes for a Fuel Tanker off New York

To reach the zone the BdU had assigned it to by January 13, U-123 sailed using its two diesel motors turning at 300 revolutions a minute. At 0448 on January 14, a light was spotted, probably the Montauk lighthouse. The weather was calm and visibility was good. In the direction of New York, the lights of Narragansett Bay were lit. At 0724 a light was spotted to port: a huge fuel tanker with all its lights on, as if in peacetime. At 0834, U-123 fired two torpedoes at a distance of 800 and 700 meters; the first, set at a depth of 4 meters, didn't explode; the second exploded under the mast after forty-five seconds, creating a flame 50 meters high and a column of smoke 200 meters high. The tanker settled, listing to starboard, but didn't sink. It sent out a message: "SOS, hit by a torpedo or a mine 40 nautical miles west of Nantucket lighthouse—*Norness* 9,577 tons gross weight." At 0853, U-123 fired the coup de grâce, and the torpedo exploded under the bridge after 107 seconds. Another loud explosion provoked a column of flames and smoke, but still the ship didn't sink. At 0910 a fourth torpedo was fired, set to a depth of 3 meters, but it had obviously malfunctioned, since the commander figured that it would be impossible to miss an unmoving target at a distance of 2,000 meters. At 0929, a fifth torpedo was fired, which exploded in the machine room after twenty-six seconds, and this time the ship sank in four minutes. With the seabed at a depth of 70 meters, the vertical stem stuck out from the surface by 30 meters; "an interesting obstacle for navigation that will force the Americans to blow it up," the commander noted. U-123 headed toward Ambrose Canal and then at 1338 dived to avoid being spotted during the day—locally, with the seven-hour time difference, this was at 0638. The commander's intention was to operate during the night between the Fire Island and Ambrose lighthouses; since the depth of the water in that sector was only 20 meters, the boat was ready to be scuttled by explosives if necessary. A radio message from the US Department of the Navy in Washington was picked up, announcing the probable torpedoing of a fuel tanker by a U-boat 60 miles south of Block Island. Sea traffic had been alerted.

The fore of the fuel tanker *Norness*, torpedoed on January 14, sticks out of the water; "a good obstacle for shipping," notes Hardegen in the logbook. *DR*

Wrecks Used as Buoys to Mark Out the Entrance to the Ports!

At 0400 the U-boat arrived close to the zone it was affected to; it remarked at least six tugs and lit-up fishing boats that took different courses, which meant that there were no mines. It drew closer—in front of it was a well-lit town that must have been a suburb of New York, whose city center was 30 miles away; the watch could see the halo of its lights above the horizon. The depth below the hull was now only 11 meters. At 0840, a larger steamer was spotted to starboard, and a torpedo was fired at 0941 at a distance of 800 meters. It exploded after fifty-eight seconds, creating a column of flame 200 meters high—the whole sky was lit up for several seconds; compared to this, the *Norness* had been a mediocre firework display, wrote the commander, before adding: "A quick coup de grâce, because this firework display must be visible from New York." At 0959 a torpedo was fired that exploded after forty-five seconds, listed backward, and sank. Because the seabed was at a depth of only 54 meters, the bows of the tanker broke the surface at an angle of 30 degrees. Hardegen wrote, "Here are some lovely buoys that we're leaving for the Yankees at the mouth of their ports to replace their lighthouses!" This was the 6,768-ton British fuel tanker *Coimbra*, which was carrying 9,000 tons of lubrication oil. At 1410 U-123 left underwater and surfaced at 2323. The U-boat was forced to crash-dive at 0001 on January 16, following the appearance of a plane. As it dropped four bombs that hit the water a long way from starboard, the commander remarked that the Americans still had a lot to learn. They surfaced at 0042. Since their presence heading west had obviously been reported, the commander decided to turn south toward Delaware Bay. In the early hours of January 17, U-123 hugged the New Jersey coast; the villages were lit up and even car headlights could be seen. At 0635, it overtook the silhouette of a destroyer on its port side. At midday—0500 in the US—a light to starboard was spotted: approaching, a freighter of about 4,000 tons was identified, heavily loaded, with just one lantern on the mast and its position lights hidden. At 1301 a torpedo was fired at a distance of 750 meters; a heavy explosion occurred under the bridge fifty-seven seconds later. The steamer began to sink while continuing its route. For a moment, only the masts were above the water, and then they disappeared too—this wreck was never confirmed by the Allies. After having to dive five times due to a seaplane, U-123 turned west toward Cape Hatteras, and a destroyer was spotted to port. At 0835 on January 18, two torpedo detonations were heard, probably coming from U-66. At 1210, the silhouette of a large fuel tanker was spotted. It was very annoying that dawn was already breaking, noted the commander; the tanker must have spotted them because it returned to the port. Then two freighters were spotted, but U-123 had to dive for the day.

The chronometer is started as the torpedo is launched—explosion! *DR*

A Knight's Cross is put together in the workshop onboard after the crew received the message on January 24 announcing the awarding of this medal to Cmdr. Hardegen. *DR*

The destruction of the Latvian freighter *Ciltvaira* pushes U-123 over the bar of 200,000 tons, of which half belongs to Cmdr. Hardegen, who notes in the logbook: "Result for the evening of January 19, 1942, a huge drumbeat with eight ships, including three fuel tankers for 53,860 tons." The next day a message from the BdU congratulates the commander: "To *Paukenschlager* Hardegen. Bravo! Very well hit." *DR*

Four Ships in One Day off Cape Hatteras

At 0304 on January 19, U-123 surfaced and spotted a light to starboard. Attack! It was a freighter weighing about 4,000 tons, heavily loaded and sailing at about 9–10 knots. Since the night was clear, the commander decided to approach close enough so that even if they were seen, the ship wouldn't be able to avoid a torpedo. It was fired at a distance of 450 meters and exploded after thirty seconds; the ship sank very fast backward, the stern touching the seabed and the stem breaking the surface. This was the 2,677-ton American freighter *Norvana*, carrying 3,980 tons of minerals; the crew of twenty-nine men didn't have time to abandon ship and were lost. Following the buoys that delimited the entrance of the port, U-123 discovered another freighter weighing about 4,000 tons. The commander decided to fire from a short distance to avoid the risk of missing with one of its last three torpedoes; there was only 7–8 meters of water under the U-boat's hull. At 0909 at a distance of only 250 meters, a torpedo was fired, set at a depth of 2 meters to avoid hitting the seabed. The torpedo broke the surface twice during its trajectory and hit the back of the ship, causing a loud explosion fifteen seconds later. The ship sank backward, rocking from side to side, which made it difficult for its crew to escape. The freighter settled on the seabed, with its chimney stack, masts, and bows above the surface. This was the 5,269-ton merchant ship *City of Atlanta*. Lights were spotted and U-123 headed north, where four freighters were seen between the U-boat and land at a distance of about 2,000 meters. Since no torpedoes were ready, the 105 mm gun was prepared. At 1034, the commander gave permission to open fire. Six rounds hit the machine room of a fuel tanker, which stopped and started to burn. Its radio sent out a message that identified it as being the 8,207-ton *Malay*. The commander hadn't realized that it was so big; it would take a torpedo to sink it, but not yet. Two other freighters sailed by but, traveling at 14–15 knots, were too fast for U-123 to get into firing position before dawn. Suddenly, a freighter of about 5,000 tons approached and passed in front of the U-boat at 9 knots. A torpedo was fired at a distance of 450 meters, breaking the ship in two. This was the 3,779-ton Latvian freighter *Ciltvaira*, carrying 6,200 tons of newspaper; two of the thirty-one crew members were lost during the attack. With this last ship, U-123 had surpassed 200,000 tons of ships destroyed, half of which while under Hardegen's command. However, a technical problem arose onboard just before firing this last torpedo at midday: because of a breach in the cooling system, one of the two diesel motors had broken down. With only one motor turning, the U-boat returned to the tanker *Malay*, which had put out the fire onboard and had sent a radio message reporting that it was functional once more. Indeed, U-123 found it sailing at a speed of 11 knots. During this time, the mechanics were actively working on replacing the damaged diesel motor's cooling system. Hardegen recounted: "This is what happens when one sends a radio message reporting that one is operational, because we can hear the 600-meter-frequency band too! We set a course of 90 degrees to return out to sea; it was already too light, diving in 10 meters of water was impossible, and there were still a number of ships around. A large fuel tanker was sailing alongside us to port, and it naturally spotted us. It tacked to try to ram us, an idea that hadn't crossed my mind. At a distance of 400 meters, with the diesel motors working at top speed and a depth of 20 meters, that made diving impossible. This was the 16,966-ton *Norwegian Kosmos II*, which we would also have liked to sink. Little by little, the distance between us increased, and after two hours it gave up the chase. Once it had reported our position heading north and it was out of sight, we changed course 160 degrees." If the mechanics hadn't repaired one of the diesel motor's cooling system in time, they would certainly have been rammed.

After all the torpedoes have been fired and the American coast was far behind them, the watch discover an isolated freighter on January 25. Attacked by gun, the *Culebra* burns. *DR*

The Knight's Cross for Hardegen

After reconnaissance around the Bermudas in the early hours of January 22, U-123 continued its route east. At 1600 on January 24, an important communiqué from the Army retransmitted aboard talked of the U-boats' great successes off the American coast, and U-123 was mentioned; in addition, at 1740, a message from the BdU announced that Cmdr. Hardegen had been awarded the Knight's Cross. During a ceremony in the control room, a Knight's Cross, made onboard, was given to the commander. Engraved behind the decoration were the words "16 ships totaling 110,209 tons." At 1431 on January 25, in the CC 7927 square, an isolated steamer was spotted. The U-boat, which found itself in the steamer's path, dived at 1702 to resurface only 600 meters behind it to open fire with the gun. Several shells exploded on the back of the ship, then under the bridge and in the machine room. But the ship replied with its 50 mm gun. After an artillery duel, the ship's gun was reduced to silence. The U-boat had nevertheless been hit by five shells, which hadn't pierced the internal hull. The freighter was burning and its crew climbed into lifeboats. The artillerymen tried a round with the 20 mm antiaircraft gun, which hadn't been working and had been repaired, but the shell exploded upon leaving the barrel, seriously wounding war correspondent Alwin Toelle, who had been taking photos of the burning ship; chef Hannes Vonderschen also received a thigh wound. Approaching the lifeboats, the commander learned from the ship's first officer that it was the 3,044-ton British freighter *Culebra*, carrying various cargo, including aircraft parts. He gave the castaways enough food to last several days, and the course for Bermuda was indicated, but in spite of this, none of the forty-nine crew members were ever found. The U-boat returned to the ship to finish sinking it with the gun and then continued east.

Because the survivors have left the ship, the gun starts up again. *DR*

The end of the British freighter *Culebra*, with its cargo containing plane parts. *DR*

The survivors of *Culebra* approach and Hardegen gives them food and directions for the Bermudas, which sadly they never reach. *DR*

On January 27, 1942, the 105 mm gun fires at a fuel tanker. *UBA*

A Second Ship Sunk by the Gun during Their Return to Base

At 0030 on January 27, a silhouette was spotted to starboard. It was quickly identified as being a fuel tanker sailing at 9–10 knots, armed with a 120 mm gun installed on a platform at the back. The U-boat approached it and opened fire with its 105 mm gun at a distance of 2,500 meters. Several salvos hit their target, causing a fire at the back of the tanker. Even though its gun had been reduced to silence, the ship replied with its machine guns on the bridge, which hit the conning tower and the U-boat's deck several times without piercing the internal hull. Shells from the U-boat set the bridge on fire. While the ship stopped to lower the lifeboats, U-123 stopped firing: Hardegen had to take care of a seaman who had been wounded in the control room. A case had fallen on him, breaking several teeth. Firing recommenced under the tanker's waterline. When all the 105 mm gun ammunition was expended, the 37 mm gun at the rear took over. After listing, the tanker broke in two, and at 0358 it sank. A freighter flying Swiss colors was seen, and the commander moved into position alongside to report the presence of castaways from the 9,231-ton Norwegian tanker *Pan Norway*, which had just sunk; the forty-one crew members were rescued. One of them was picked up by the U-boat and transferred to the neutral ship. Without any munitions, U-123 continued on its route toward Lorient, which it reached at 1500 on February 9, with flat batteries and only 80 liters of fuel left. A large crowd had gathered to greet the new "Ace," whose highly successful patrol had been cited by the radio. *Vizeadmiral* Karl Dönitz was also there and personally awarded the Knight's Cross to Hardegen.

After sinking *Pan Norway*, U-123 goes looking for a neutral ship nearby so that it can pick up the survivors. In 1981, Norwegian survivor Wilfred Larsen, saved from the sinking fuel tanker by U-123, met with Reinhard Hardegen. A moving meeting between two men that history had made enemies so many years ago.

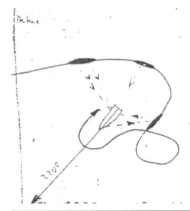

Schema of the attack on the tanker with the gun; taken from the logbook. *UBA*

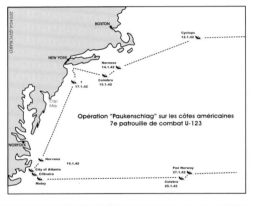

Itinerary of U-123 off the American coast during Operation Paukenschlag. *A. Guychard*

The Norwegian fuel tanker *Pan Norway* is the last ship to be sunk during the seventh patrol. *DR*

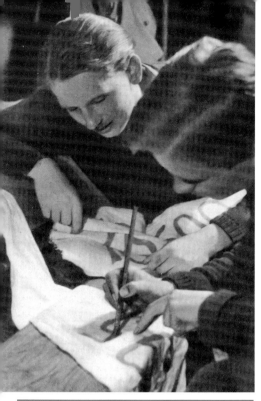

Victory pennants are made while crossing the Atlantic. *DR*

Before arriving in Lorient, Hardegen raises the ten pennants to the top of the periscope. *DR*

Painting the Knight's Crosses won by commanders Moehle and Hardegen. *DR*

The conning tower is decorated with the homemade Knight's Cross, attached to the wave breaker. A drumbeat has been painted on, with the estimated total tonnage sunk written below it. The fins from the shark caught off Africa hang from the antenna wire. In the middle of the photo is IWO Rudolf Hoffmann, who will be disembarking to take command of U-845. *Wolfgang Ockert*

U-123 approaches the pontoons on the Scorff. *LB*

The ten pennants (*from the top*): four fuel tankers—the first is *Coimbra* (6,768 tons; overestimated at 10,000 tons), then *Norness* (9,577 tons), *Pan Norway* (9,231 tons), and the *Malay* (8,206 tons), which had been damaged but didn't sink; next are the freighters—*Cyclops* (9,076 tons), *City of Atlanta* (5,269 tons; underestimated at 5,000 tons), then a pennant with the number 4,000 for an unidentified ship lost on January 17 but not confirmed by the Allies, *Norvana* (2,677 tons; overestimated at 4,000 tons), *Ciltvaira* (3,779 tons; overestimated at 4,100 tons), and *Culebra* (3,044 tons). The announced total is ten ships sunk for 66,134 tons; the reality is eight destroyed for a total of 49,421 tons, which is considerable but shows the difference in the estimation by over 15,000 tons for one mission. Multiply this by the number of missions carried out by each U-boat; this explains why the BdU overestimated the Allied losses. *LB*

On the right: IIWO Schroeter, decorated with the Iron Cross 1st Class the following day. *UBA*

On February 9, 1942, U-123 is the first U-boat to return from the American coast. *UBA*

The scene is filmed by a war correspondent; it will be shown in all the cinemas throughout Europe during the newsreel before the main feature. *LB*

On U-123's deck, *Vizeadmiral* Dönitz, helped by his aide-de-camp, hangs the Knight's Cross around Cmdr. Reinhard Hardegen's neck. *Charita*

Reinhard Hardegen will be considered a national hero in Germany. *Charita*

In the center: chief of U-boat operations of the BdU, *Fregattenkapitän* Godt. *UBA*

Several officers have come onto U-123's deck to congratulate Hardegen: on the left is *Korvettenkapitän* Hans-Rudolf Rosing, chief of the Central Department of the BdU; in the middle is Herbert Kuppisch, officer from the BdU's general staff. *Charita*

Certificate of the Knight's Cross awarded to Reinhard Hardegen. *Andreas Dwulecki*

The day after his arrival and after a party with the entire crew, Reinhard Hardegen returns to participate in the medal-awarding ceremony for members of his crew. *LB*

The commander of U-123 has made the front page of a French magazine. *LB*

And the German newspaper *Die Kriegsmarine*. *Thierry Nicolo*

A Fuel Tanker Sunk 335 Mile Northeast of the Bermudas

At 2210 on March 2, 1942, U-123 left Lorient for its eighth war patrol. For the forty-eight hours it took to cross the Bay of Biscay, the U-boat remained submerged during daylight. This precaution was now necessary due to the presence of Allied planes. On March 22, after twenty days sailing west without incident, U-123 arrived in the CB 9355 square, 335 miles northeast of the Bermudas. At 1047, the watch spotted smoke on the port side. Approaching, a fuel tanker was identified, sailing at about 8 knots and seeming to zigzag on the waves. Since the wind was getting stronger, with a force 4–5 sea, the commander decided to attack straightaway. At 1706, the U-boat dived to get into firing position and immediately fired a torpedo set at a depth of 3 meters from the aft tube, but it missed its target. A second was fired at a distance of less than 500 meters. After eighteen seconds, a metallic noise was heard, not the real explosion that the crew was used to hearing, especially at this short distance. Had the torpedo malfunctioned? But the commander was at the periscope, and when he was able to see the ship again, it was rapidly sinking backward. At 1802 they surfaced and the commander quickly climbed the ladder to the conning tower and saw that the back of the ship was already underwater. The bows were rising higher and higher, and it sank in sixteen minutes. When he questioned the survivors, he learned that this was the 7,034-ton American tanker *Muskogee*, transporting 67,265 barrels of heavy crude oil, which was the reason why it hadn't caught fire.

Joining the German navy in 1933, Hardegen passed his pilot's license two year later. In 1936, a crash put him into the hospital for six months. In October 1941, Dönitz was informed that the wounds sustained during the crash made Hardegen unqualified for the U-boat service. He had one leg slightly shorter than the other and stomach problems, the latter of which meant he had to eat specially prepared, easily digestible food. His medical dossier had arrived too late to stop him from embarking, because he had already left on mission or to another base. Thanks to good results during his first patrols, Dönitz exceptionally authorized him to carry out two supplementary patrols. *LB*

Preparing to leave for the American coast on March 2, 1942, Horst von Schroeter had been promoted to IWO; the new IIWO is Wolf-Harald Schuler. *LB*

Board games while crossing the Atlantic for the American coast. *From left to right*: Engineer-in-Training Mertens, IWO Schroeter, "Hardi," Midshipman Rudi Holzer (who will be killed during the duel with USS *Atik* on March 27), and LI Schulz. *UBA*

Chef Hannes Vonderschen, treated for a leg wound, has returned to his job. U-123 sails submerged during the day while crossing the Bay of Biscay. *LB*

The Gun Ends Up Setting a Fuel Tanker on Fire

At 1823 another tanker was spotted, zigzagging irregularly at a speed of about 10.5 knots. It was still an hour and a half before dusk. After having approached to 500–600 meters, U-123 prepared to launch a torpedo set at a depth of 3 meters, which, due to an error of manipulation, got stuck in the tube. The U-boat turned round to fire a torpedo from the aft tube. But when the ship was only 300 meters away, its watch spotted the U-boat and the tanker tacked 180 degrees to starboard. While Hardegen waited for another favorable moment, he heard that the torpedo had been fired from the aft tube without his order. The seaman had fired it manually, believing that he had heard "*Los.*" The torpedo hadn't been primed and was lost. The 8,138-ton tanker *Empire Steel* reported the U-boat's position by radio. Built in 1941, this modern tanker was armed with an 88 mm gun at the back, two 60 mm guns on each side of the chimney stack, and, on level with the upper deck, spotlights and machine guns. Now the U-boat was opposite its front, and the ship zigzagged even more to get out of its way

and advanced at 12 knots. The commander didn't want to get too close because of the guns, and at 0301 a salvo of two torpedoes were fired from a distance of 900 meters. After sixty seconds they exploded under the foremast, creating a loud, heavy explosion, and the watch could see nothing but a sea of flames. Just as they thought that the ship had sunk, it put out signals once more. Thanks to the fire extinguishers, the fire had been limited to the foredeck and the engines still worked. At 0341, U-123 fired six 105 mm shells at the machine room and three others at the back of the ship, where the munitions should be stocked; now the entire ship was on fire and then it listed to port. The bows rose 20 meters into the air, which showed off the hole made by the torpedoes. At 0956, only five hours later, it sank with its cargo of 11,000 tons of kerosene bound for England. The commander remarked that it was incredible that it hadn't fired a single shell from its guns during the entire attack, and that the crew had obviously been badly trained. After diving at 1427 following the appearance of a seaplane, U-123 continued to advance underwater throughout the afternoon; with a sea at force 6–7 and an opposing wind, it went faster underwater than it would have on the surface.

On March 24, 1942, the fuel tanker *Empire Steel* bursts into flames after being hit by two torpedoes. *DR*

Duel with a U-boat Trap Warship

The U-boat continued its route west, and at 2303 on March 26, smoke was seen to starboard. It wasn't a convoy, as the watch first thought, but a single isolated freighter that was regularly giving off great columns of smoke. Was the 3,209-ton American freighter *Carolyn* acting as a Q-ship—a U-boat trap? However, when U-123 cautiously approached on the surface, the commander discovered a completely ordinary freighter, apparently without an added superstructure. At 0237 on March 27, the U-boat fired a torpedo at a distance of 650 meters, which exploded under the foredeck. The freighter caught fire at the point of impact, settled a little, and listed to port. It gave out its name and position by radio. The U-boat approached from behind, and the watch saw that two lifeboats were lowered into the water. Up until then, everything was normal. But the commander discovered that the freighter continued to advance at a reduced speed and that the distance between the two of them was being reduced. The U-boat tacked to starboard, and the ship copied it. Suddenly the freighter, whose hidden arms on the bridge had been uncovered, opened fire with at least a big gun and two 50 mm machine guns. The bullets hit the conning tower and whistled past the heads of the submariners; Midshipman Rudi Holzer was wounded and lowered into the control room. U-123 moved away at top speed, with the advantage of being hidden by the heavy smoke coming from its diesel motors.

Suddenly a large object flew overhead, and just afterward loud explosions rocked the U-boat. The commander recounted: "We saw great sprays of water, and it was obvious that the freighter had launched depth charges at us. I had been taken in like a beginner by a heavily armed U-boat trap!" Once the U-boat was out of firing range, the damage report was that the midshipman had taken a bullet that had torn his thigh open. He was losing a lot of blood, and his situation was without hope; he was given morphine for the pain and lost consciousness at midnight. The conning tower had sustained eight bullet impacts, but the U-boat remained waterproof. The commander decided to attack underwater; he thought that the holds must be full of a special cargo that allowed the ship to remain on the surface, but in fact they were full of wood pulp. At 0429 on March 27, a torpedo was fired that exploded in the machine room twenty-four seconds later. The front of the ship sank to the bridge, the back rose out of the water, and the propeller could be seen. The crew took up place in the lifeboats. When the U-boat surfaced at 0550, the freighter was still in the same position. Suddenly there was a heavy explosion, either the boiler or the depth charges and munitions, and the ship sank without leaving a trace. This was indeed an American warship, the freighter *Carolyn* transformed into a U-boat trap under the name of USS *Atik* (AK101); none of its crew survived, probably due to the bad weather. Midshipman Holzer died during the underwater attack, and he was buried at sea after a short ceremony.

Often after being hit, fuel tankers, although on fire, manage to reach a port. *DR*

A Fuel Tanker Damaged and the U-boat Pursued by a British Motor Torpedo Boat

On March 28, U-123 approached the American coast. The following day was spent immersed. After the U-boat fired two torpedoes that malfunctioned due to their gyroscopes not working properly, the commander, to avoid wasting fuel during the day so close to the coast, which was watched from sea and sky, decided to head southeast. They reached the DC 1244 square on April 1, but only a small coastal cruiser and a plane were spotted. At 0542 on April 2, a fuel tanker sailing at 11 knots was spotted and pursued on the surface. At 0718 the U-boat dived and fired a torpedo; because the electrical firing system wasn't working, it was fired manually three seconds later. But in spite of the distance of only 500 meters, it didn't explode. The commander thought that the ship's hull was protected by netting. At 0721, U-123 surfaced to fire its gun at a distance of 2,500 meters. Over the course of thirty-five minutes, numerous shells exploded on the ship's deck, which started to burn, in the machine room, on the front of the tanker, and at the back, notably under the waterline, since apparently it was sailing with ballast. Its crew climbed into lifeboats. Suddenly the slender silhouette of a small warship was seen heading straight for the U-boat. At 0755, the commander ordered a crash dive; in less than

five minutes, he thought they had time to fire a torpedo to sink the tanker once and for all. While he had his mind on the antitorpedo netting, the warship passed above the U-boat and dropped a depth charge, which exploded just behind the stem. The commander looked through the periscope and saw a U-boat hunter a few meters away; it had sailed above them and was now turning around (in fact it was the British motor torpedo boat HMS *MTB-322*). Because of the calm sea, it must have seen the periscope, and it tried to ram the U-boat. The commander remarked that they were dealing with beginners, who hadn't armed the depth charge properly at this depth of only 30 meters; the damage was insignificant. Through the periscope, Hardegen could see men on the deck of the U-boat hunter, which was turning back and arming other depth charges. He lowered the periscope, and the U-boat descended to 20 meters. The warship passed above them once more, but nothing happened, and the commander thought that lowering the periscope was enough to make the enemy believe that the U-boat had been sunk during the first pass. It didn't have Asdic, and U-123 was able to escape without making any noise. After an hour and a half of sailing using the electric motors, the commander could see the burning tanker through the periscope. Damaged but not sunk, the 7,057-ton American tanker *Liebre* was boarded once more by eight crew members eight hours after the attack; it managed to reach a port on April 4, where it was repaired before going back into service on July 19.

On April 8, the fuel tankers *Oklahoma* and *Esso Baton Rouge* are damaged by a torpedo. Their back ends are on the shallow seabed; they will be refloated. *Texaco Archives*

New Ships Torpedoed off the Florida Coast

The U-123 headed southwest in the direction of Charlestown. Ship traffic seemed to have been interrupted; apparently the freighters remained in the port during the night. The U-boat continued south in the direction of the St. Johns River to Florida; along the coast, all the lights were on, as if it was peacetime. Two fuel tankers and a freighter were finally spotted on April 8. At 0752 the 9,264-ton tanker *Oklahoma* was the first to be hit by a torpedo, which exploded in the machine room; it sank backward with its stern on the seabed. At 0844 a torpedo was launched at the second fuel tanker, which had sailed closer to the coast; this also exploded in the machine room. This was the 7,989-ton American fuel tanker *Esso Baton Rouge*, which also sank backward to the seabed at a depth of 13 meters. In the logbook, Hardegen wrote: "We are starting to specialize in fuel tankers—this is the tenth we have sunk with our boat." U-123 returned toward *Oklahoma*, whose stem was sticking out of the water, and fired a few rounds of 105 mm shells so that it would take on more water and sink completely; it started to burn, but the two tankers would nevertheless be refloated and would be back in service by the end of the year. In the early hours of April 9, the watch thought that they had spotted freighters, which lit their navigation light intermittently, but eventually realized that they were car headlights on the coastal roads. At 1716, the 3,365-ton American freighter *Esparta* was sunk. At 0422 (2122 local time) two days later, the 8,081-ton American fuel tanker *Gulfamerica*, lit up by the lights of Jacksonville, Florida, was hit by a torpedo and sunk by twelve 105 mm shells. Hardegen wrote: "The torpedo found its target after 177 seconds; the enormous explosion, like a giant torch, lit everything up like it was full daylight; a rare spectacle for the tourists at the resort, who were probably having dinner at the time!"

Badly Damaged by a Destroyer

At 6056, U-123 slipped between a fuel tanker and a freighter. It was suddenly forced to crash-dive because a plane had spotted it and had fired off a flare; the U-boat hit the seabed at a depth of only 20 meters. It surfaced at 0717, and a message from the freighter giving their exact position was picked up—it must have seen the U-boat in the light of the flare. It was time to move away, noted the commander. At 0815, a silhouette was spotted to starboard, heading straight for the U-boat. Hardegen recounted: "I could attack. But while we were tacking, a plane launched another flare and we were completely lit up. The silhouette was then identified as a destroyer, which exchanged a signal in Morse code with the plane. The flare was still working, and to starboard I spotted another plane without lights on. I ordered the engines to be stopped, hoping that it hadn't spotted us, but suddenly it tacked and headed straight for us. Alarm! When I fell into the conning tower, it was right over us but miraculously didn't drop a bomb. While we dived to 30 meters, we could hear the sounds of propellers as the destroyer came closer and closer. When it passed above our heads we could hear the disagreeable sounds of six depth charges dropping into the water. The U-boat shook horribly and the men were tossed every which way; anything that wasn't fixed down fell over. Smoke and whistling sounds were everywhere, breathing equipment was prepared, and the secret coding materiel started to be destroyed. Then it came back; we were settled on the seabed at a depth of 22 meters, and

The 8,081-ton tanker *Gulfamerica*, torpedoed and hit by several shells from the 105 mm gun off Jacksonville, Florida, on April 11, will sink five days later. *NA*

On April 11, U-123 escaped depth charges while it was at a depth of only 22 meters; Hardegen's worst souvenir. The damages are repaired. *DR*

On April 13, since there are no more torpedoes onboard, U-123 sinks the freighter *Korsholm* with its gun. *DR*

everything that worked had been turned off. But even though the destroyer passed above us, it didn't drop another bomb. We must have been leaking air because we could hear bubbles forming outside. After an hour, the destroyer moved away—it was incredible that it didn't have Asdic; all it needed to do was to drop another series of depth charges in the same place as the first by following the bubbles, and we would have been forced to surface." The damage was repaired little by little—half the batteries weren't working as well as one of the two diesel motors; in addition, because some valves had been destroyed, the boat wasn't operational for a crash dive. The essentials were repaired.

Oak Leaves for Hardegen

At 0511 on April 13, the 2,609-ton American freighter *Leslie* was sunk by the last torpedo, the fiftieth fired by Reinhard Hardegen as commander. At 0745, U-123, not having any more "eels" onboard, sank another freighter with its gun 70 miles off Cape Canaveral, Florida: the 2,647-ton Swedish *Korsholm*. According to his calculations, Hardegen remarked that U-123 was the second U-boat in this war to have surpassed the mark of 300,000 tons of ships sunk. His radioman sent the following message to the BdU, composed in verse: "Seven fuel tankers have seen their final hour. U-boat trap sank them slowly. Two freighters are resting with them on the seabed. Sunk by one who took up a drum beat!" Then he announced their return to base to the crew. They had a stock of only twenty-nine shells for the 105 mm gun, which had to be taken out from their place under the upper deck. For the last ship destroyed during this patrol, U-123 positioned itself at a distance of only 400 meters on a parallel course to its target. Using the 105 mm gun, the aft 37 mm gun, and even the 20 mm antiaircraft gun in the "bath," it sank the 4,834-ton American freighter *Alcoa Guide* on April 17. With no more ammunition, U-123 continued on its way home, with a reported result of eleven ships sunk representing 79,649 tons (in truth, eight ships sunk for 39,917 tons and three damaged for 24,310 tons). On April 23, a radio message announced that Cmdr. Hardegen would be adding the Oak Leaves to his Knight's Cross. They reached Lorient at 1050 on May 2, 1942. On May 16, it left again for a total overhaul in Germany. U-123 would be taking a dangerous route, particularly above the British Isles. It had to dive on numerous occasions following the appearance of planes and escaped four well-dropped bombs on May 21. After calling at Bergen and then Kristiansand, Norway, U-123 arrived in Kiel on May 29, flying forty-five pennants representing 304,974 tons.

The homebound journey is announced to the crew; theoretically, the submarine has passed 300,000 tons of ships sunk. Richard Amstein, a.k.a. Kraxel, plays the accordion. *DR*

On April 23, Radioman Fritz Ralalski receives the message announcing that Oak Leaves have been added to Reinhard Hardegen's Knight's Cross. *DR*

The German newspapers announce Cmdr. Hardegen's success off the coast of Florida. *UBA*

On May 2, 1942, a huge crowd has come to welcome U-123 returning from its second patrol off the American coast. *LB*

While crossing the Atlantic, the petty officers play Skat. *DR*

Before their arrival, Richard Hardegen, with a part of his crew, poses in front of the 105 mm gun; the five silhouettes and the tonnage of the freighters sunk by the gun between January and April 1942 have been drawn on it. The estimation of tonnage sunk by this U-boat since it was put into service has been painted on the conning tower: 304,975 tons. *Wolfgang Ockert*

Approaching Lorient, the commander chats with war correspondent Rudi Meisinger, who participated in the combat mission.

This time U-123 has brought back eleven victory pennants. It is the most effective patrol in the number of ships hit and tonnage sunk: 64,277 tons. *UBA*

Female army auxiliaries welcome U-123. *LB*

The A3 pontoon isn't big enough to hold everyone who has gathered here: shipyard workers, land personnel, nurses, musicians, and submariners. *LC*

The pennant on the bottom represents the U-boat-trap ship USS *Atik*, sunk on March 27. *LB*

The commander is interviewed in the presence of Viktor Schutze, the chief of the 2nd Flotilla. *LB*

Reinhard Hardegen, with his charts and plans, goes to give his report on the patrol. *LB*

Oak Leaves have been added to Hardegen's Knight's Cross.

The 105 mm gun with the five freighters that it sank between January and April 1942. *LB*

War correspondent Meisinger adjusts *TMech* Heinz Halling's Iron Cross. *UBA*

Portrait of the commander with his Knight's Cross with Oak Leaves. On May 7, 1942, he will receive the U-boat War Badge with Diamonds. *UBA*

On May 5, 1942, Admiral Erich Raeder, commander in chief of the Kriegsmarine, arrives in Lorient and salutes U-123's crew, and in particular Rudolf Muhlbauer, known for having the best eyes in the German U-boat Corps. *Charita*

Passage at Aarhus in Denmark; in the center of the photo is Hardegen, and in front of him is IWO Schroeter, who will succeed him. *LB*

U-123 leaves for Germany for a complete overhaul. *LB*

Arriving in Kiel on May 29, 1942. *UBA*

Both of the periscopes have been raised to hold the forty-five pennants representing 304,975 tons. *UBA*

Kapitän zur See Friedeburg, second in command at the BdU, salutes U-123's crew. *DR*

On May 31, the crew members of U-123 are warmly welcomed in Bremen. *LB*

Cmdr. Hardegen and friends. *LB*

Book written by Reinhard Hardegen about his patrols, published in February 1943. *LB*

Visiting Bremen Zoo, on the left is *Oberleutnant zur See* Schroeter, who will become U-123's commander on July 31, 1942. *LB*

The crew members are welcomed to the mountains for their leave. Young women offer a bouquet of flowers to Cmdr. Hardegen. *LB*

Peaceful games at the ski resort, far from the storms in the Atlantic. *LB*

Hardegen will receive a first position on land on August 1, 1942, as training officer at the 27th U-boat Flotilla. After March 1, he will be responsible for training submariners at the school in Flensburg-Murwik. *DR*

Departure from Kiel on December 5, 1942. The new commander, Horst von Schroeter, has had his naval officer's promotion emblem painted onto the conning tower: the Crew 37b, a vertical glaive in a black shield. Meteorologist Dr. Georg Rakuttis has been embarked; he is in charge of sending out regular weather reports on the radio, notably by using pilot balloons. *LB*

Horst von Schroeter, only twenty-two years old, has been successful in his first mission as commander. He is seconded by *Leutnant zur See* Schüler, who had been IIWO during Hardegen's last patrol. The new IIWO is Josef Monikes, and the LI is Reinhardt Konig. *UBA*

In a Wolfpack against a Convoy

After being completely repaired and having a Metox plane-radar-detecting system, U-123 restarted training exercises in the Baltic Sea: attacking in a wolfpack, firing torpedoes. A large part of the crew had been changed, as well as the commander and all his officers, and the new crew had to learn to work together as a team. The U-boat left Kiel on December 5, 1942, for its ninth combat patrol. At 1600 on December 20, a radio message from the BdU assigned U-123 to the Spitz wolfpack; it would be taking up the role of scout in the AL 8541 square, off the British coast. Nothing was seen until December 24, when the U-boat dived for a short ceremony celebrating Christmas. At 1820, two days later, a radio message reported the presence of a convoy heading west. After a forty-eight-hour search to the southwest, the ONS-154 convoy, heading from Liverpool to New York, was found at 1709 on December 28. It disappeared with dusk; however, at 2302 two ships that appeared to be abandoned were discovered. Two torpedoes were fired, the first exploded on one of the two unmoving wrecks. The 3,385-ton British freighter *Baron Cochrane*, carrying charcoal and already damaged an hour and a half earlier by a torpedo from U-406, sank in six minutes. The success of the second torpedo, which the crew heard exploding after a trajectory of seven minutes, was never confirmed by the Allies. Another isolated ship from the convoy was discovered. At 0500, U-123 fired a salvo of three torpedoes at this big ship,

The CAM ship *Empire Schackelton*, 7,068-ton merchant ship, torpedoed by U-123 on December 29, is sunk a short time afterward by the gun onboard the nearby U-435. *DR*

already damaged by two torpedoes from U-225 just before midnight the night before. One of them exploded on the hull, just below the foredeck, after a trajectory of five minutes, thirty-five seconds; the 7,068-ton British CAM ship (an armed merchantman equipped with a plane catapult) *Empire Schakelton* stopped its engines and sank backward, water reaching to the bridge. Suddenly, while U-123 was maneuvering, the shape of another U-boat appeared: U-435, which immediately started firing its gun at the wreck. It completely sank forty-two minutes later, taking with it 2,000 tons of diverse cargo and 1,000 tons of munitions. Onboard this ship was the convoy chief, Vice Admiral Wion de Malpas Egerton, who was saved along with the sixty-eight other crew members. The pursuit had taken U-123 northwest of the Azores. After being resuplied by U-463 and transferring a sick crew member on January 3, 1943, U-123 headed northwest to reach its new operations sector off Newfoundland and take up its role as scout for the Jaguar wolfpack. On the way a second resupply meeting with U-117 took place on January 10, and it reached the BC 2546 square five days later. For nine days the ocean was empty. At 1229 on January 24 in the AJ 5566 square, due to having a fuel stock that was down to 35 square meters, the commander gave the order to return to base. After crossing the Atlantic from west to east, the U-boat reached Lorient at 1115 on February 6. U-123 had sailed 8,501 miles, of which 635 were submerged.

Stock is taken in the control room at the beginning of January 1943. The pursuit of the convoy has taken U-123 northwest of the Azores; it will now turn toward Newfoundland. *UBA*

February 6, 1943: U-123 arrives in Lorient with two pennants. *UBA*

Helmsman Walter Kaeding on watch duty in the conning tower at the beginning of the patrol in the Spitz wolfpack, west of the British Isles. *Charita*

Their former barracks having been destroyed by bombs, U-123's crew is taken by bus to Lager Lemp, an R&R camp in the country. The evening after their arrival, British bombers return in higher numbers to Lorient: 296 planes, which drop 254 tons of bombs. *LB*

Following in the wake of its escort, U-123 will pass in front of Port-Louis Citadel. Arriving on the Scorff on February 6, the crew discovers a totally different landscape to the one they knew before its last departure from Lorient in May 1942. The U-boat is quickly put into shelter in a concrete cell. *LB*

Last Wolfpack Attack Too Difficult: A Dive to 180 Meters

At 1700 on March 13 1943, U-123 left Lorient for its tenth combat patrol and headed for the Spanish coast. After several alerts for planes and three destroyers, it reached the Canary Isles on March 22 and then sailed along the African coast. To economize on fuel, navigating on the surface was carried out with one diesel motor and one electric one. At 2100 on March 27, it reached its position as scout in the Seerauber wolfpack in the DU 2194 square. The following day a convoy was reported by two U-boats a little farther south of its position, and the two diesel motors were pushed to top speed. At 1325, two freighters and an escort ship were spotted, but an hour and a half later one of the merchant ships suddenly exploded, hit by the torpedo from another U-boat. At 1844, U-123 dived to attack; through the periscope, the commander watched the approaching freighter and corvette. When the corvette was only 1,000 meters away, the crew heard the characteristic sound of Asdic, which, to their dismay, had just been switched on. When the corvette was 250 meters away, the commander ordered a rapid dive deeper. Three depth charges exploded quite nearby without causing any damage inside,

and the U-boat descended to a depth of 180 meters and escaped. Once on the surface, it was discovered that the no. 1 ballast had been torn open, and it had to be bailed out every hour. However, U-123 pursued the convoy and was obliged to dive several times when its antiplane radar system went off. At 1717 on March 29, a plane dropped three bombs, which exploded when the U-boat was at a depth of 40 meters. The sustained damage couldn't be completely repaired quickly: the top of the UZO aiming optics' support was badly damaged and the firing system was no longer operational. During the night of March 29–30, after unfruitful attempts to attack and six alarms due to the regular passage of Allied planes based on land, the commander noted that the crew was exhausted. At 1435, U-123, along with the other U-boats in the Seerauber wolfpack, received a radio message ordering it to give up the pursuit of this convoy, which was decidedly very well protected. At midnight, the BdU directed it to a new operations sector south of Freetown. It could now hunt as a lone wolf—the tiring convoy attacks in a pack were over. At 1441 on March 31, it had to crash-dive following the appearance of a seaplane close by, but no bombs were dropped. It surfaced at 1701 and dived again at 1925, when the watch spotted an approaching seaplane, which dropped three bombs far enough away to cause no damage except for a few smashed lightbulbs and blown fuses. The tear in the no. 1 ballast was repaired by April 2.

Certificate of crossing the equator on April 15, 1943. *UBA*

On March 13, 1942, U-123 leaves Lorient for the African coast. In front of it is U-161; the two U-boats follow in the wake of escort ships to avoid risks from mines. *LB*

A British Submarine Sunk off Freetown

At 0501 on April 8, after having to let several neutral freighters go by, a target was spotted off the French Guinean coast, in the ET 2167 square. After approaching, no name or national flag was seen that could identify it. A salvo of three torpedoes were fired; two exploded and the ship sank in three minutes. U-123 surfaced to talk to the survivors—who spoke in Spanish. This was the 3,972-ton neutral freighter *Castillo Montealegre*. The following day, a message from the BdU, which had been advised of the incident, ordered the crew to keep the whole affair a secret—the order was finally rescinded on April 19 following a new message from the BdU specifying that the torpedoing should be noted in the logbook. After crossing the equator on April 14, U-123 arrived close to Freetown Port four days later. At 0344, two shapes were spotted by the watch—a minesweeper and a British submarine out on exercises. At 0534 two torpedoes were fired at the minesweeper from a distance of 3,000 meters, but they missed their target. A second salvo of two torpedoes, fired at 0647 from a distance of 1,500 meters, also missed. The tubes were reloaded and a fifth torpedo was fired at the minesweeper at 1153—another miss. But one of the two following torpedoes fired in the direction of the submarine exploded: HMS *P-615* sank with its crew of forty-four men. The minesweeper, which seemed invulnerable and had cost five torpedoes for nothing, had moved away, doubtless to act as an escort for a freighter that had been spotted during the approach and that U-123 prepared to attack. At 1239 a first torpedo was fired at the merchant ship, and it exploded after 280 seconds, a distance of 4,200 meters. The freighter, estimated as weighing 5,500 tons, listed only slightly; a second torpedo was fired at 1351 and exploded on the front, accentuating the list. A third torpedo was fired at 1419; this time it exploded in the center of the ship. The 7,459-ton British freighter *Empire Bruce*, full of linseed, sank in one minute; its crew of forty-nine men was picked up by the minesweeper.

The watch on U-123 scrutinizes the horizon; machine guns are ready for action in case of an aerial attack. However, this is supposed to be avoided thanks to the Metox radar detector, whose fragile wooden retractable antenna can be seen; this has been nicknamed Biscaye Kreuz (Cross of Gascony) by the crew. *LB*

Watch duty off the African coast; in the center is IWO Wolf-Harald Schuler. *LB*

The British submarine HMS *P-615* is sunk off Freetown on April 18, 1943. *DR*

The Last Three Ships Sunk by U-123

In the evening of April 19, U-123 received a radio message from the BdU, giving it a free choice in where it wanted to operate. Cmdr. Schroeter decided to go farther south. At 2200 on April 24, after reaching the FF 1796 square, U-123 turned back northward. At 1944 on April 29, a large isolated freighter was spotted in the EU 7245 square, sailing at 12 knots. At 2324, two torpedoes were fired; after seventy-two seconds, one of them caused a loud explosion in the front of the ship, and the crew of thirty-two men evacuated the ship (they were later saved). At 0001 on April 30, a third torpedo that was fired missed its target, but the ship, which had risen into a vertical position, sank on its own, bows first. This was the 5,931-ton Swedish freighter *Nanking*, out of Bombay for Liverpool with a cargo of 8,500 tons of kyanite, peanuts, and cotton. On May 5, the 4,566-ton British freighter *Holmbury* was stopped by a torpedo and was sunk by twenty-six shells from the 105 mm gun. Its master was taken aboard as a prisoner. On May 9, 60 miles south of Monrovia, the 6,244-ton British freighter *Kanbe* was hit by two torpedoes and sank in two minutes: this was the last ship sunk by U-123, whose commander announced the return to base to his crew on May 13. Five days later, the U-boat received food and fuel from U-460 in the FD 2223 square, west of Freetown, and a new Metox radar detector was also transferred to it. On May 30, a party was held onboard to celebrate the U-boat's third commissioning anniversary. Three days later a Portuguese freighter was spotted—the eleventh neutral ship seen during the patrol. U-123 reached Lorient at 1830 on June 8, 1943, after 11,967 miles covered, with 731 submerged.

U-123 approaches *Holmbury*, which is sinking after being hit by twenty-six shells from the 105 mm gun. *UBA*

Holmbury disappears; it is the fifth ship sunk during this patrol. *UBA*

On April 19, U-123 continues its course south. *LB*

The British freighter *Holmbury* is stopped by a torpedo on May 5; the artillerymen get ready to sink it with the gun. *LB*

Holmbury lifeboat approaches U-123. *LB*

Horst von Schroeter talks to John Bryce Lawson, master of the freighter, who will be taken aboard as a prisoner. The rest of the crew manages to reach Liberia. *LB*

The dinghy carrying foodstuff is pulled toward U-123. *LB*

The crew will be able to improve its menu. *LB*

On June 8, 1943, Lorient comes into sight; the men's beards have grown a great deal since March 13. *LB*

On May 18, 1943, U-123 receives supplies from the XIV-type U-460. *LB*

U-123 has covered 11,967 miles during its tenth patrol. IWO Wolf-Harald Schuler disembarks; he will become commander of U-720 and survive the war. *UBA*

Like the other crew members, the commander has put on his life jacket for the few hours of navigation on the surface after Point "Latern," the place where its escort to Lorient waited for it. *LB*

After about three months off the African coast to Freetown, five ships and one submarine have been sunk, representing 28,855 tons. *UBA*

Firing at a Convoy off Guiana

Now equipped with a quadruple 20 mm antiaircraft gun on a platform behind the conning tower, U-123 left Lorient on August 1, 1943, along with U-68, U-505, and U-523, to be able to reply as a group to an aerial attack. Three days later a radio message from the BdU ordered the U-boat back to Lorient to be equipped with the new Wanze-Hagenuck type of radar-detecting system that had just been delivered to Lorient; specialists had discovered that the old Metox apparatus gave out parasite waves that could guide a plane straight to the U-boat. U-123 left again on August 16 in the direction of the Gulf of Guinea. On August 23, while it was sailing submerged at a depth of 80 meters in the CG 1356 square, it was depth-charged by two destroyers, which ended up abandoning the pursuit. On August 28, a radio message from the BdU ordered it to cross the Atlantic to the ED 90 sector above the coast of Guiana. The U-boat reached north of South America on September 11. After long, monotonous days, a convoy was spotted on September 21 in the EP 4484 square: four columns of twenty-three ships with fuel tankers in the fore, followed by Liberty ships. On the starboard side, where the U-boat was positioned, two modern destroyers were seen acting as escorts. U-123 slipped between the two destroyers and fired four torpedoes at the Liberty ships, and detonations were heard after one minutes, fifty seconds, as well as at five, six, and seven minutes, but there were no signs of wrecks through the periscope. Had two freighters been hit? The U-boat turned and fired two torpedoes from the aft tubes; the detonations were heard after eight minutes. No loss was ever confirmed by the Allies. After twenty days of unfruitful search, a radio message from the BdU on October 12 informed them that being resupplied was no longer possible and that they should return to base. The commander calculated that he needed 70 square meters of fuel to reach Lorient—there was 73 square meters stocked. To economize and take fewer risks, the journey would be made submerged to a depth of 60 meters, using a single electric motor, during the day, and coming to the surface at night, coupling a diesel motor and an electric one.

A telegram received on September 6 announces the awarding of the German Cross in Gold to Helmsman Walter Kaeding, who has been present aboard since the first patrol. *UBA*

After reaching the African coast, U-123 turns west to cross the Atlantic. *LB*

Departure from Lorient on August 16, 1943, for the eleventh patrol, and faces are tight. *From left to right*: Cmdr. Horst von Schroeter, No. 1 Seaman Heinz Diegnitz, and *ArMechGast* Riedel. *Leutnant zur See* Josef Monikes has been promoted to IWO, and the new IIWO is *Leutnant zur See* Klaus-Christoph Marloh. *UBA*

After weeks of watch duty without result, a convoy is finally spotted north of Guiana on September 21, 1943. The torpedoes that were fired miss their target. *LB*

On October 23, during the return trip, U-123 dives to escape from a light cruiser southeast of the Azores. This is the first unsuccessful mission for the submarine. *LB*

Arriving in Lorient on November 7, 1943, after the attack by a Tsetse Mosquito, the body of the fatally wounded *Bootsmannsmaat* Günther Struve is brought back to land. *UBA*

Depth-Charged and Then Attacked by a Plane on the Day It Arrived

At 2150 on October 23, in the DH 1192 square southeast of the Azores, the slender silhouette of a warship was spotted to port, probably a small cruiser, which must have detected the U-boat because it was heading straight for it. At 2151, after having tried to outdistance the ship, a crash dive was ordered when the ship was only 2,000 meters to port. While the U-boat was descending to 30–40 meters, four depth charges exploded, two of which were quite close. In silence the U-boats heard Asdic being turned on to find them. They escaped once again; the commander couldn't explain the presence of this isolated ship in the middle of the ocean. At 2034 on October 24, an Aphrodite decoy balloon was released and the U-boat moved away, tacking 6 degrees every ten minutes. On November 7, 1943, U-123 was a few hours away from its arrival in Lorient. It had crossed the Atlantic both ways and had been on operation for nearly three months. Since 0535 that morning, it had been sailing peacefully on the surface, everyone

thinking about what he would do once on land. At 0943, a plane suddenly flew out of the clouds and sped toward the U-boat, which didn't have time to dive. With its six 20 mm antiaircraft guns, it opened fire at the plane at a distance of 2,000 meters. It was a Mosquito "Tsetse" from the RAF's No. 618 Squadron, armed with a 57 mm gun—its first attack against a U-boat. The plane fired eight shells, which hit the water at first, and then one of them exploded against the conning tower. Bootsmannsmaat Günther Struve was fatally wounded and two other crew members were also wounded; Helmsman Kaeding was the only person in the conning tower not to be hit. The plane was already banking for a second attack; the DCA began to fire while it was at 2,500 meters, and this time the oil reservoir was hit. Its 57 mm gun jammed and it could fire only with its machine guns, then it banked again and turned southwest with smoke coming from it. Because of an 18-by-6.5-centimeter hole in the conning tower, the U-boat was unable to dive. Following an urgent radio message sent by the U-boat, four Luftwaffe Junkers Ju 88 aircraft flew out to protect it, and then two torpedo boats from Concarneau arrived. Everything was over by 1648; U-123 was put into shelter in the small U-boat base on the Scorff River.

Awarding the DKG to the commander and to Reinhardt Konig in December 1943. *UBA*

Ceremony for awarding the German Cross in Gold—DKG—to Walter Kaeding by the FdU-West *Kapitän zur See* Rosing in Pignerolles. *UBA*

Last Attack by a Destroyer

Equipped with a Naxos-Borkum detecting system and armed with several Zaunkonig T5 acoustic torpedoes specially created to fight against warships with light draft, U-123 left Lorient on December 29, 1943. Following a number of technical problems discovered during a test dive, it had to turn back the following day. It left for its twelfth combat patrol on January 9, 1944, heading for the Gulf of Guinea. In contrast to the past, it spent one and a half times longer submerged than on the surface. Each day of navigation was carefully set: toward 0300, it dived and sailed at a depth between 50 and 60 meters until 1400, when it rose to periscope depth and surfaced at 2000 only to recharge its batteries. In this manner it advanced at only about 100 miles a day, two-thirds of the time on the surface and the rest submerged. At this speed it would reach the African coast on January 22, and the Gulf of Guinea on February 12. After ten days, no traffic having been seen in this sector, the commander decided to turn west. At 0016 on February 29 in the EV 7285 square, 60 miles from Takoradi, a plane was spotted at 1,500 meters and the U-boat dived. It resurfaced at 0137, but the Naxos radar detector was sounding and it dived and sailed submerged. At 0218, the hydrophone signaled the approach of a warship, and soon the sounds of its Asdic could be heard: a "ping" every three seconds and then a "ping" every 1.3 seconds and then every second. U-123 descended to 180 meters. At 0329 ten depth charges exploded; at 0342 U-123 changed course 340

degrees and released a Bold decoy to create a mass of air bubbles. At 0415, there were no more Asdic sounds—the destroyer had left. U-123 continued its patrol toward the Liberian coast. At 1700 on March 10 in the EU 4885 square, a Catalina seaplane was seen, and at 1755 a small convoy comprising one ship escorted by two destroyers was spotted. Arriving underwater to a distance of 1,000 meters, an escort ship turned on its Asdic; at 1811, U-123 fired a salvo of three torpedoes at the ship and then, three minutes later, fired a T5 acoustic torpedo at the nearest destroyer and then tacked to port. The four torpedoes missed their targets, exploding at the end of their trajectories between eleven and fifteen minutes later. Obliged to dive once more because of the Catalina, the commander thought that a new attack would be impossible. At 2000 he announced their return to base to the crew. On March 21, an isolated tanker was pursued for several hours, but its speed of 14 knots was too fast for the U-boat. In the evening of March 29, U-123 received fuel and foodstuff from U-488 in the EG 6539 square, west of the Cape Verde Islands. It then turned toward Lorient, which it reached at 0700 on April 24. During its patrol, 11,656 miles had been covered: 9,124 miles during 995 hours on the surface, and 2,532 miles during 1,539 hours submerged. On June 1, 1944, the Knight's Cross was awarded to *Oberleutnant zur See* Horst von Schroeter for having participated in six paytols as an officer aboard U-123 before becoming its commander and having sunk six ships and a U-boat. Suffering from the wear and tear of 720 days at sea, U-123 was decommissioned on June 17, 1944.

U-123 leaves Lorient on December 29, 1943, for its twelfth combat patrol.

Allied planes have won the battle for the ocean, so the twelfth patrol will be carried out submerged from 0300 to 2000 every day. U-123 surfaces at night only to recharge its batteries. Crew members are in the fore compartment, with the torpedo-launching tubes in the background. *UBA*

It takes over a month to reach the Gulf of Guinea, where no traffic is seen for ten days. *LB*

U-123's electric-motor compartment. *UBA*

On March 10, only a small convoy is spotted, comprising a freighter escorted by two destroyers and watched over by a Catalina. U-123's attack is unfruitful. *LB*

Cmdr. Schroeter hasn't had a success in spite of 107 days at sea, U-123's longest patrol. But reaching Lorient on April 24, 1944, is already exceptional. *UBA*

Chief engineer Reinhardt König, decorated with the Knight's Cross on July 8. *UBA*

On March 21 an isolated fuel tanker is seen, but it is too fast for U-123. *LB*

R&R camp Lager Lemp and a ceremony for awarding the Knight's Cross to Walter Kaeding on May 15, 1944. On October 1, he is promoted to Leutnant zur See. *UBA*

Rudolf Muhlbauer, the only *Maat* in the Kriegsmarine to be awarded the Knight's Cross, carried out fourteen patrols aboard U-123 and U-170. He spent 822 days at sea and took part in the destruction of 309,500 tons of ships. His particularly excellent sight saved his boat twice. *UBA*

Cmdr. Horst von Schroeter is awarded the Knight's Cross on June 1, 1944. At the beginning of July 1944, he relaxes at Lager Lemp with his officers and petty officers. *UBA*

U-123's insignia has been used as U-2506's emblem. *UBA*

U-123's crew manages to reach Germany by train just before the Allies encircle Lorient. *Kapitänleutnant* Schroeter took command of the XXI-type U-2506, just out of the shipyards, on August 31, 1944. *Charita*

Before Lorient could be surrounded by the American forces coming from Normandy, U-123's crew left for Germany on a train. On August 31, 1944, Horst von Schroeter was given the command of the XXI-type U-2506. This modern U-boat, just out of the shipyards, never had an operational career; it was handed over to the British in Bergen on May 9, 1945. The next day U-123 was captured by the Navy, following the surrender of the Lorient pocket. Repaired by the French, it put out of Keroman on July 6, 1946. On June 23, 1947, U-123 was officially renamed *Blaison*, as a homage to Captain Georges Blaison, former commander of the Free French Navy's submarine *Surcouf*. It enjoyed a long career in the French navy, which took it to Toulon, Casablanca, Oran, Alger, Ajaccio, Brest, Cherbourg, Le Havre, Bordeaux, Saint-Nazaire, Lorient, Nice, and Bizerte under seven different commanders. It was placed on special reserve in Toulon on August 1, 1957, and condemned on August 18, 1959. Used as a target boat at the entrance to the Gulf of Saint Tropez, it sank on September 10, 1959, in waters about 250 meters deep—its position is 43°17'05"N and 06°48'15"E.

† † †

U-123's first commander, Karl-Heinz Moehle, died in 1996, and its third commander, Horst von Schroeter, died in 2006. Reinhard Hardegen, the last U-boat captain to wear the Knight's Cross with Oak Leaves, died on June 9, 2018, aged 105.

U-2506 is handed over to the British on May 9, 1945, in Bergen, Norway. *UBA*

On May 15, 1945, at Adelby cemetery near Flensburg-Murwik, *Korvettenkapitän* Hardegen, wearing the uniform of commander of the 1st Battalion of the 6th Navy Infantry Regiment, participates in the funeral of the commander of the navy school, Wolfgang Luth. *UBA*

At Norheim Sund on July 6, 1945, Horst von Schroeter says goodbye to his crew. *UBA*

Ceremony at Keroman I on July 6, 1946, with U-123 done up by the French navy. *ECPAD*

Under the French flag, U-123 goes out to sea for trials. *ECPAD*

In Lorient on May 10, 1945, U-123 is discovered intact in cell no. 3 in Keroman I by the Franco-American Liberation Forces. *NA*

Renamed *Blaison* on June 23, 1947, the submarine leaves Lorient for Toulon. *DR*

Blaison's insignia. LB

During the first meeting of former German submariners in Hamburg on May 15–16, 1954, the twenty-two former members of U-123 represent the biggest delegation. *UBA*

Reunion of the former crew members of U-123 at U-Boot Archiv in Cuxhaven in the 1990s. On the bottom left is Reinhard Hardegen, who celebrated his 102nd birthday on March 18, 2015; in the center is Horst von Schroeter, who died in 2006. *UBA*

The new shape of *Blaison*, with the bathtub's walkway free of antiaircraft materiel. The new number, S 611, was painted on the conning tower while it sailed from Casablanca to Toulon in July 1953. *DCAN Lorient*

BIBLIOGRAPHY AND ACKNOWLEDGMENTS

Bibliography and Sources

Busch, Rainer, and Hans-Joachim Röll. *Der U-Boot Krieg, 1939–1945*. 5 vols. Hamburg, Germany: Mittler Verlag, 1996–2003.
Dörr, Manfred. *Die Ritterkreuzträger der U-Boot-Waffe*. Osnabrück: Osnabrück Biblio-Verlag, 1988.
U-123 logbook.
Websites: https://U-boat.net and http://uboatarchive.net

Acknowledgments

Horst Bredow, creator of U-Boot Archiv in Cuxhaven; Josef Charita, Wolfgang Ockert, and Thierry Nicolo; Proofreading: Monique, Alain Durrieu, and Lucien Le Pallec.

This book is dedicated to the victims of the ships sunk by U-123.